1000 STRANGE BUT TRUE ANIMAL FACTS

This edition published by Parragon Books Ltd in 2014 and distributed by

Parragon Inc.
440 Park Avenue South, 13th Floor
New York, NY 10016
www.parragon.com

Copyright © Parragon Books Ltd 2014

Edited by Grace Harvey
Cover design by Francesca Winterman
Production by Jonathan Wakeman
Designed, produced, and packaged by Tall Tree Ltd

ISBN 978-1-4723-4646-9

Printed in China

Discovery KIDS™

1000

STRANGE BUT TRUE ANIMAL FACTS

PaRragon

Bath · New York · Cologne · Melbourne · Delhi
Hong Kong · Shenzhen · Singapore · Amsterdam

CONTENTS

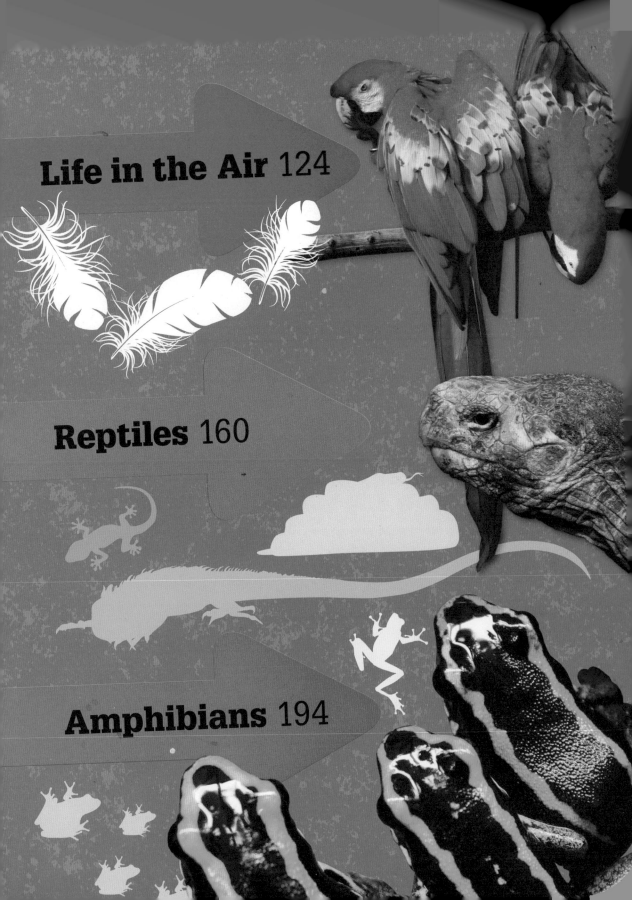

LAND
MAMMALS

CHAPTER 1

GIBBONS
can cover 50 feet
in **one swing**
using their long arms.

That's the length of five
small cars lined up ...

... end to **end.** #0001

8 MONKEY FACTS

South American monkeys have tails that can grip. They use their tails like a fifth limb as they swing through the trees. #0002

Monkeys live in groups called **troops**. Each monkey has allies and enemies within the troop. #0003

Capuchin monkeys make different sounds to warn their troop-mates of different predators. They have one sound for snakes, another for leopards, and another for eagles. #0004

Female baboons will **adopt** youngsters whose mothers have been killed. #0005

Howler monkeys have booming voices that can carry up to **3 miles** through the forest. #0006

Squirrel monkeys **rub their feet with their own urine**. As they walk around, they mark their territory with the smelly pee. #0007

Studying rhesus monkey blood helped scientists to work out the different blood groups that humans belong to. #0008

Monkeys went into space before people did. A rhesus monkey called Albert II was the first, in 1949. #0009

10 FACTS ABOUT APES

Apes are large primates with no tails and big brains. **Humans are a species of ape.** #0010

Newborn chimps have a tuft of white fur **on their bottoms.** #0011

Families of gibbons **SING SONGS** together while they sit in the trees. #0012

The name "orangutan" means "person of the forest" in Malay. #0013

Chimpanzees and bonobos are the closest relatives to humans. #0014

The orangutan is the largest fruit-eating **animal** in the world. #0015

CHIMPS are poor swimmers, but they do wade through **SHALLOW WATER.** They hold their arms above their heads as they do so. #0016

10

Mountain gorillas live in the high mountains of central Africa. They have **extra-thick fur** to keep them warm. #0017

GORILLAS are the largest **PRIMATES.** #0018

An adult male can weigh **440 POUNDS—** that's heavier than two adult humans. #0019

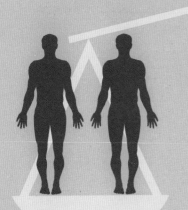

7 FACTS ABOUT Cats

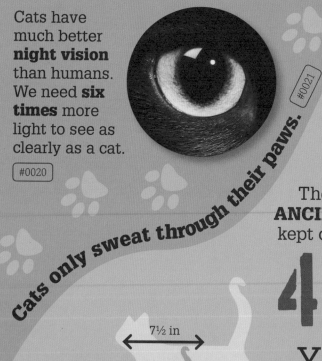

Cats have much better **night vision** than humans. We need **six times** more light to see as clearly as a cat.

#0020

Cats only sweat through their paws.

#0021

Cats purr when they are ill. The vibrations may help their bones and muscles to heal.

#0022

The **ANCIENT EGYPTIANS** kept cats as pets nearly

4,000 YEARS AGO.

#0023

7½ in

2¾ in

The **smallest adult cat ever measured** was a **Himalayan-Persian** called **Tinker Toy,** which was only **2¾ inches** tall and **7½ in** long— about the size of a rat. #0024

There are currently

55

recognized **breeds** of house cat.

#0025

Cats sometimes **chew grass** to make themselves **throw up fur balls.** #0026

12

6 BIG CAT
FACTS

The **cheetah** is the **fastest land mammal,** and can accelerate from **0 to 60 miles per hour** in just 3 seconds. That's the same as an F1 racing car. #0027

Most **jaguars** are orange with black spots, but about **6 percent** are black all over. #0028

A lion's **ROAR** can be heard from **5 mi** away. #0029

Tigers are known to imitate the sounds of other animals to lure in prey. #0030

Tigers now inhabit only 7 percent of the areas that they lived in **100 years ago,** because humans are taking over their land. #0031

LIONS do most of their **HUNTING** at night. #0032

13

12 DOG
FACTS

Mongol ruler Kublai Khan kept **5,000** dogs. `#0033`

Domestic dogs walk in a circle before they lie down, as their wild ancestors would have done to flatten the ground. `#0034`

Greyhounds have been recorded **running at 45 mph**—that's nearly twice as fast as top human sprinters. `#0035`

A Dalmatian puppy is born completely white. The first spots appear after about three weeks. `#0036`

All dogs have a see-through third eyelid that gives their eyes extra protection. `#0037`

Puppies are born blind, deaf, and toothless. #0038

A dog's sense of smell is up to

100,000

times more sensitive than a human's. #0039

Its wet nose traps chemicals in the air, helping the dog to smell them. #0040

Dogs have 18 muscles in their ears. #0041

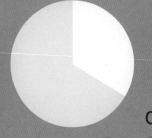

Dogs drink water by forming the back of their tongue into a cup to scoop the water up. #0042

The tallest dog is the Great Dane. The biggest of all, called Zeus, stood **44 in** from **paw to shoulder**—as tall as an average five-year-old child. #0043

About ⅓ of all homes in the world have a pet dog. That's about

half a billion

doggie homes. #0044

7 DEER FACTS

The smallest species of deer, the **South American pudu,** stands less than **16 in tall**— about the height of a wine bottle.
#0045

The largest deer is the elk (also known as a moose). It stands up to 6½ ft tall. #0047

The **CHINESE WATER DEER** does not have antlers. The males grow **TUSKS** instead. #0046

Male deer use their bony antlers to fight one another over the **FEMALES.** This is called **"RUTTING."**
#0048

A deer's antlers fall off every year, and the deer **grows a new set.** #0049

The only female deer to grow antlers are **reindeer. They use them to clear away the snow** when feeding in winter.
#0050

Reindeer migrate farther than any other land mammal, traveling up to **3,100 MI** a year in search of **FRESH PASTURES.**
#0051

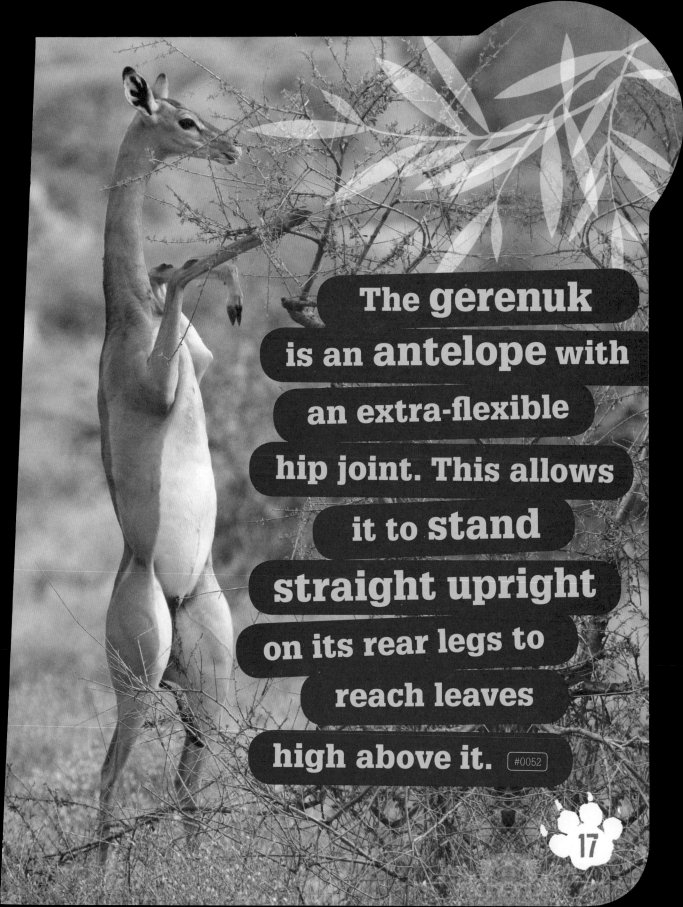

The gerenuk is an antelope with an extra-flexible hip joint. This allows it to stand straight upright on its rear legs to reach leaves high above it. #0052

17

9 HORSE FACTS

Horses sleep standing up. #0053

A horse's height
is measured in **hands**.
One hand equals 4 in.
#0054

A **PONY** is a horse that is
under 14.2 hands tall. #0055

The oldest recorded horse
was called **OLD BILLY**.
He lived to the age of 62.
#0056

18

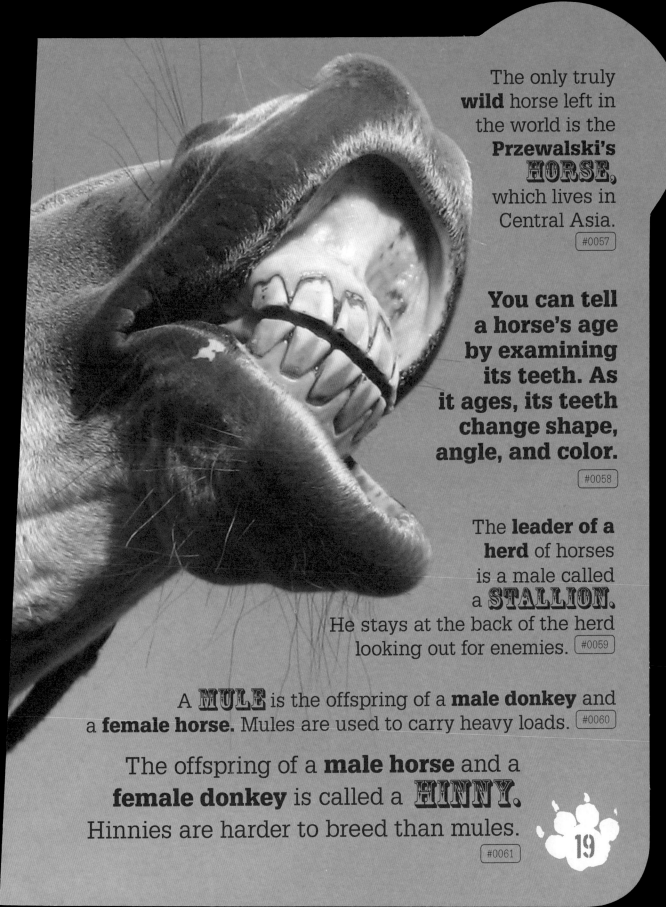

The only truly **wild** horse left in the world is the **Przewalski's HORSE,** which lives in Central Asia. #0057

You can tell a horse's age by examining its teeth. As it ages, its teeth change shape, angle, and color. #0058

The **leader of a herd** of horses is a male called a **STALLION.** He stays at the back of the herd looking out for enemies. #0059

A **MULE** is the offspring of a **male donkey** and a **female horse.** Mules are used to carry heavy loads. #0060

The offspring of a **male horse** and a **female donkey** is called a **HINNY.** Hinnies are harder to breed than mules. #0061

5 CAMEL FACTS

A camel's hump is **FULL OF FAT.** When there is no food, it can live off its fat reserves for several months without eating. #0062

There are more than **1 million** wild camels in **Australia**. They were introduced to the continent by humans in the **19th century.** #0064

Camel's milk contains
10 **times** as much iron as cow's milk. #0063

A camel can drink **35 GALLONS** of water in just **15 minutes.** #0065

A **BACTRIAN CAMEL** can carry a load of 550 lb for **four days** without stopping. That's more than the weight of three adult humans. #0066

6 GIRAFFE FACTS

20 ft. #0067

The giraffe is the **tallest land animal**, standing as high as

The giraffe has a **blue-black** tongue that is nearly 20 in long. #0068

Giraffes can **run at 35 mph** in short bursts. #0069

Sometimes a giraffe will rest with its head bending back to its body. #0070

To get enough blood **up its long neck** to the brain, a giraffe has to **pump blood twice as hard as other large mammals.** #0071

MALE GIRAFFES
fight each other by **smashing their heads** against one another's body. #0072

21

10 FACTS ABOUT
MONOTREMES

Monotremes are **the only mammals that LAY EGGS.**
#0073

There are just **two kinds** of monotreme alive today: the **platypus** and the **echidna.**
#0074

A platypus eats **20 percent** of its own body ......

PLATYPUSES ARE BORN WITH TEETH, but they drop out when they are young. Adults grind their food using horny plates in their mouths. #0076

The platypus's bill can detect **electrical signals** in the bodies of its prey. This allows it to **HUNT AT NIGHT UNDERWATER.** #0077

Male platypuses have **venomous spurs** on the backs of their feet. #0078

An echidna mother **LAYS JUST A SINGLE EGG** each **breeding season.**

#0079

A young echidna is called a **PUGGLE.**

#0080

The mother **digs her puggle a burrow** and **leaves it there,** returning every five days to feed it.

#0081

....➤ weight in food every day.

#0075

When it feels threatened, an echidna **curls up into a ball,** protecting itself with its **sharp spines.**

#0082

9 MARSUPIAL FACTS

Marsupials are mammals that **give birth to tiny, helpless babies** that develop in their mother's **pouch.** Examples of marsupials include kangaroos, koalas, and quolls. #0083

A baby marsupial that lives in its mother's pouch is called a **JOEY**. #0084

A newly born quoll joey is the size of a **grain of rice.** #0085

All the mammals that are native to Australia are **MARSUPIALS.** #0086

Opossums are immune to most

snake venom. #0087

Koalas feed on **eucalyptus leaves,** which are **low in nutrition,** meaning that koalas have **little spare energy.**

#0088

To save energy, koalas sleep for up to 18 hours a day.

#0089

Wombat poop is **cube-shaped.**

#0090

The feisty **TASMANIAN DEVIL** has pink ears, but they go red if you make the marsupial angry.

#0091

25

6 FACTS ABOUT KANGAROOS

The red kangaroo is the **LARGEST SPECIES** of kangaroo. It can weigh more than

220 LB

—as much as a baby elephant.

#0092

Kangaroos can't hop **<<<BACKWARD** because their large, muscular tails are in the way.

#0094

A red kangaroo can leap a distance of 29 ft in a **single hop.**

#0033

Male kangaroos fight each other in "**boxing matches.**"

They stand on their hind legs and try to push each other over.

#0095

Kangaroos can jump to a height of more than 6½ ft.

#0096

Although they have been known to **ATTACK PEOPLE,** there is only one recorded human death caused by a kangaroo.

#0097

27

10 ELEPHANTS
FACTS ABOUT

There are **two kinds** of elephant: **African** and **Asian**. African elephants have much bigger ears. Their big ears keep them cool on hot days. #0098

Just as we are left- or right-handed, elephants are left- or right-tusked. The dominant tusk is usually more worn down than the other. #0099

Female African elephants have a gestation (pregnancy) that lasts **22 months**—longer than any other animal. #0100

Elephants use mud or sand as sunblock. #0101

Elephants have **26 teeth**, which are usually replaced **6 or 7 times in their life.** They eat plants, and wear their teeth out through chewing. #0102

An elephant's heart beats only **25 times per minute**—about three times more slowly than the average human heart. #0104

Elephants lift and spread their ears to signal to other elephants when they are alarmed. #0103

An African elephant's trunk is about **6½ ft long.** #0106

Female elephants spend all their lives with their family group. **Each group is led by an old female called the**

matriarch.
#0105

Elephants can communicate by **stamping on the ground.** Other elephants sense the vibrations many miles away. #0107

29

9 FACTS ABOUT HIPPOS

The name "hippopotamus" means **HORSE OF THE RIVER** in Greek. #0108

An **adult** hippo can weigh more than **3 tons**— as much as a medium-sized **elephant.** #0110

Hippo milk is **bright pink**. #0109

A hippo's eyes are covered with a special clear membrane. The **membrane acts like goggles** to help the hippo see underwater clearly. #0111

Nearly **3,000** people are **killed by hippos** every year. #0112

Hippo skin is **16 IN THICK.** #0113

The closest living relatives to hippos are actually **whales.** #0114

Its **HUGE** canine teeth are used for **fighting not eating.** #0115

Hippos can **sleep underwater.** They bob up to the surface every few minutes to take a breath **without waking up**. #0116

30

5 RHINO
FACTS

Rhinoceroses can grow up to **11½ ft long**—as long as two adult humans lying toe to toe. #0118

There are only around **40** JAVAN RHINOS **left on the planet.** #0119

Rhinos are very rare because humans hunt them. Nearly **700** were killed in South Africa in 2012. #0120

Rhinos welcome oxpecker birds because they **eat the itchy parasites** that live on the rhino's skin. #0117

A rhino's **horn** is made from keratin, the same stuff that our fingernails and hair are made from. #0121

14 FACTS ABOUT RODENTS

About **40%** of all mammal species are rodents. #0122

There are more than 2,000 species of rodent. #0123

A mouse can **SQUEEZE** through a gap just **¼ in WIDE** —about the width of a pencil. #0125

Rodents have **four big front teeth.** The teeth never stop growing, and must be kept worn down by gnawing. #0124

A mouse's tail is **as long as the rest of its body.** #0126

The capybara's EYES, NOSE, and EARS are all right at the top of its head. This allows it to swim with just the **top of its head above the water.** #0127

The capybara is the largest rodent, **weighing up to 146 lb**—about the same as an average adult human. #0128

Naked mole rats can live for up to 20 years. #0129

The naked mole rat spends its entire life in **underground tunnels.** #0130

Naked mole rats never develop cancer. Scientists study them to find out why this is. **IT MAY HELP US TO FIND A CURE.** #0131

Naked mole rats can **run backward** just as quickly as they run forward. #0132

A naked mole rat digs tunnels with its front teeth. It can **seal off its mouth completely** as it digs to stop dirt from getting in. #0133

GUINEA PIGS are active for up to 20 hours a day. #0134

Flying squirrels **glide from tree to tree**, using flaps between their legs like the **wings of a glider.** #0135

5 FACTS ABOUT RATS

Rats can tread **WATER** for three days. #0136

RATS regularly **EAT** their own **POOP.** #0138

A rat can survive being washed **down a sewer.** #0137

There are **as many RATS AS PEOPLE** in the U.S. #0139

A **rat can fall** from a height of **50 ft**— about the height of a three-story building—and still land safely. #0140

4 FACTS ABOUT BEAVERS

Beavers can gnaw through tree trunks up to **3 ft** in diameter.

#0141

A beaver's home
is called a **lodge.** Beavers build their lodges in lakes, and the lodge can only be **entered from underwater.**

#0142

A beaver has a
FLAT TAIL
that acts like a rudder, helping it to **steer as it swims.**

#0143

Beavers often create their own lakes by **damming streams.** The longest beaver dam ever found was **930 yd long.**

#0144

35

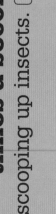

11 FACTS ABOUT ANTEATERS, ARMADILLOS, AND SLOTHS

A giant anteater's **tongue** is longer than its head. It has **tiny hooks** on it to **catch insects.** #0145

The anteater uses its **huge claws** to dig into termite and ant nests. #0147

The giant anteater eats **35,000** insects every day. #0146

An anteater flicks its tongue out **three times a second,** scooping up insects. #0148

NINE-BANDED ARMADILLOS
always give birth to **four identical quadruplets**—something no other **mammal** is known to do. #0149

Armadillos find their way around **at night** using **little hairs** on their sides and belly known as **CURB FEELERS.** #0150

Sloths hang from **branches** using their long, curved claws. They sometimes **don't fall off** even when they die. #0152

On the ground, sloths **cannot walk**. They drag themselves along with their **front arms.** #0153

Sloths come to the ground **once a week to poop.** #0154

Sloths can move more easily in **water** than on the ground, and may **swim from one tree to the next.** #0155

37

6 FACTS ABOUT WEASELS, STOATS, AND MINKS

The weasel can take down prey **ten times its own weight.** #0157

Weasels need to eat **a quarter of their own body weight** of food every day. #0158

The fur of a weasel **turns white in the winter** to hide it against the snow. #0156

Stoats are **strong swimmers,** and have been known to swim for more than half a mile. #0159

The American mink **hisses** when it is threatened, and **purrs** when it is feeling contented. #0160

Mink are fast swimmers, and will hunt fish that are bigger than themselves. #0161

39

5 FACTS ABOUT OTTERS

When hunting **UNDERWATER,** otters use their sensitive whiskers **to detect vibrations** in the water caused by moving **FISH.** #0162

An otter can close its **EARS** and **NOSE** to keep out the water when **DIVING.** #0163

The South American giant otter can grow up to **5½ ft long**—the same as an adult human. #0164

Z Z z z z z z Z Z Z Z Z Z z Z

Sea otters

sleep in the water. They often hold onto each other's paws so that they don't drift away. #0165

A sea otter has the
THICKEST
fur of any animal.
It has as many hairs on
0.15 square inches
of its skin as we have on
our **whole head—** 150,000. #0166

41

9 FACTS ABOUT BEARS

During late summer and early fall, GRIZZLY BEARS EAT CONTINUOUSLY **without getting full.** They eat as much as they can to get fat for the winter. #0167

All bears share the same ancestor—the dawn bear, which lived more than 20 million years ago. #0168

The **spectacled** bear gets its name from the **circular marks** around its eyes, which make it look like it is **wearing spectacles.** #0169

The brown bear is the **largest and heaviest** of all bears, weighing as much as **1 ton**—the weight of a small car. #0170

Female grizzly bears can lose **40 percent** of their body weight over the winter. #0171

Over a short distance, a grizzly bear can **outrun a horse.**

#0172

Sun bears **love honey ...**

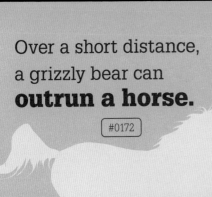

... they will rip open tree trunks ...

... in search of **beehives.**

#0173

Polar bears are very strong swimmers, and have been seen more than **60 mi** from land.

#0174

Grizzly bears usually give birth to

TWINS.

The cubs will stay with their mother for **two years** before going off on their own.

#0175

43

9 MEERKAT FACTS

A group of meerkats is called a **mob,** and can include as many as **40 animals.** #0176

In a mob, just one dominant pair breeds. The dominant pair is called the **alpha pair**. #0177

The dark patches around a meerkat's eyes lessen the glare of the sun. #0178

Meerkats can eat poisonous scorpions. They pluck off the stinger quickly before tucking in. #0179

Young meerkats are taught how to do this by the adults. #0180

44

As they forage, the meerkats take turns to be sentries. The sentries keep watch, standing on their hind legs to look out for eagles and other predators. #0181

When the sentries call out, the meerkats run for their burrow. #0182

One mob may have up to five different burrows. #0183

Adults take it in turns to stay in the burrow looking after the newborn pups. #0184

9 FACTS ABOUT BATS

Bats are the **only mammals** that can **FLY.**
#0185

The flying fox isn't actually a fox—it is the largest bat, with a wingspan of **5 FT.** It is also called a **FRUIT BAT.**
#0186

A bat's wing is **so thin** that you can see the **blood vessels** running through it.
#0187

A bat's knees

bend the opposite way

from human knees. This makes it easier for them to run on all fours.
#0188

Bats make high-pitched sounds and listen for the echoes in the dark. This is called **echolocation**. The sounds are too high-pitched for us to hear, which is just as well as they are as loud as a jet engine. #0189

Emitted sound of bat

Reflected echo of prey

A brown bat can catch over **600 INSECTS** in **1 hour**. #0190

Vampire bats feed on the **BLOOD OF MAMMALS.** The bats bite their victims while they are asleep, and lick the wound. #0191

Fruit bats big eyes do not use echolocation, but have to help them see in the dark. #0192

The tube-lipped nectar bat's **tongue is 1.5 times longer** than its **body.** It uses it to reach into plants and collect nectar. #0193

47

LAND MAMMALS FACTFILE

BIG AND SMALL

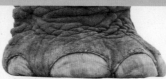

Elephants are the **LARGEST** land mammals. They can weigh over **6 tons** but spread their weight over **four large feet,** so they barely leave footprints. #0195

The SMALLEST mammal is the bumblebee bat, which weighs just 0.07 oz—the weight of a small coin. #0194

A walrus's tusks may be up to **3¼ FT LONG.** #0196

An adult giraffe's legs alone are about 6 ft long— **taller than most humans.** #0197

WARM AND HIDDEN

Mammals are all **warm-blooded.** #0198

Sloths move so **SLOWLY** that algae grow on their fur. The green algae help to hide the sloths in the trees. #0199

During a cold year, a dormouse will stay asleep for more than **6 months.** #0200

A polar bear appears white from a distance, but its hairs are transparent. #0201

Prairie dogs live in a network of underground tunnels called **a town.** A prairie dog town can cover an area of 250 acres—**as big as a human town.** #0202

The Weddell seal spends most of its life under the sea ice in Antarctica. It keeps breathing holes in the ice open by gnawing the ice away with its teeth. #0203

REPRODUCTION

The Virginia opossum has a gestation period of just **12 days**. #0206

MAMMALS are the only animals that produce milk. #0204

All mammals have  **HAIR** when they are born. #0205

A newborn panda is SMALLER than a mouse. #0207

WEIRD BUT TRUE

BADGERS POOP in special latrines some way from **their setts.** #0208

In New Zealand there are about **7 sheep** to every person.  #0209

Some species of shrew are **poisonous.** #0210

An elephant's trunk contains **40,000** muscles. #0211

HYENAS have huge hearts, making up about  **10** percent of their body weight. #0212

A hyena's bite is so **strong** that it can **CRUNCH** through elephant bones. #0213

CHAPTER 2

CORAL REEFS
cover less than
0.1 percent
of the
world's
oceans,

LIFE IN THE SEA

25 percent

yet they are home to

of all **marine species.**

#0214

4 DEEP-SEA MONSTER FACTS

The **gulper** eel's HUGE MOUTH allows it to swallow prey that is BIGGER than itself.

#0215

The **vampire squid** has the **largest eyes** of any animal compared to its body size.

#0216

The **anglerfish** makes its own light, which it uses to tempt fish near enough for it to strike.

#0217

The **giant squid** grows up to **46 ft** in length— longer than a bus.

#0218

4 GIANT CLAM
FACTS

Giant clams can weigh up to **440** lb— nearly as much as three adult humans.

#0219

They can measure **4 ft across.**

#0220

Giant clams are **hermaphrodites,** meaning that they are both

MALE AND FEMALE.

#0221

A **giant clam** can live for up to 150 years. #0222

11 FACTS ABOUT
SHARKS

Sharks can detect a single drop of **blood** in an Olympic-sized swimming pool full of **water.**

#0224

The smallest shark is the **dwarf lanternshark.** It is just **8 in** long. #0223

THE
WHALE SHARK
is the biggest fish in the world, growing up to 40 ft long—60 times longer than the dwarf lanternshark.

#0225

A shark's **skeleton** is made of **bendy cartilage** (the same stuff your nose is made from), **not bone.** #0226

If a shark **stops** swimming, it **sinks,** as it does not have a swim bladder to help with buoyancy. #0227

SHARKS
have been swimming in the oceans for **400 MILLION** years—since before the dinosaurs.

#0228

A **GREAT HAMMERHEAD**

shark's eyes are **3¼ ft** apart.

#0229

54

A great white's bite is **three times** more **powerful** than the bite of a **lion.**

#0230

On average, **1,000 people a year are killed by bees.**

#0232

On average, fewer than **ten people** a year are killed by great whites ... but more than 1,000 people a year are killed by bees.

#0231

A **GREAT WHITE** shark needs to eat **11 TONS** of food a year—equivalent in weight to 150 people.

#0233

3 DOLPHIN FACTS

Dolphins only put half of their **brain** **to sleep at a time.**

This allows them to stay swimming and keeps them from drowning. #0234

The **Ganges river dolphin** is almost blind. It lives in muddy rivers, where eyesight is not much use. #0235

23 ft

Some dolphins can jump **23 ft** out of the water. They could jump right over an adult giraffe.

#0236

56

4 facts about the
KILLER WHALE

Despite its **name,** the killer whale is actually a **species** of
dolphin.
#0237

Killer whales eat more than
100 lb
of food a day. #0238

A killer whale's brain is **five times larger** than a human
BRAIN. #0239

Killer whales live in **family groups** that contain four different generations—from youngsters to their great-grandmothers.
#0240

57

8 MIGHTY WHALE FACTS

Bowhead whales can live for up to **200 years**— the longest lifespan of any mammal. #0241

Humpback whales **sing to each other**. A humpback whale's song can be heard by other humpback whales **thousands of miles away**. #0242

Sperm whales have **no sense of smell**. #0243

Sperm whales **dive** to depths of **up to 1.8 mi** in search of food. #0244

SPERM WHALE

58

Sperm whales **feed on giant squid**. The whales often have scars from battles with the squid. #0245

BOWHEAD WHALE

The bowhead whale has the **largest mouth of any animal**. It measures **up to 13 ft** from top to bottom when open.
#0246

Unlike other whales, the beluga whale has a **flexible neck** that allows it to turn its head in all directions. #0247

BELUGA WHALE

HUMPBACK WHALE

The male narwhal has a **swordlike spiral tusk** that grows up to 9 ft long.
#0248

NARWHAL

7 BLUE WHALE FACTS

The blue whale is the **BIGGEST ANIMAL** that has ever lived, at up to **100 FT** long. #0249

It weighs **150 tons**

as much as **24 elephants.**

#0250

Its heart weighs **1,320 lb,** and is the size of a small car. #0251

It can eat **up to 4 tons of krill** in one day. #0252

A baby blue whale puts on about **200 LB** in weight per day for the first year of its life. #0253

Its **TONGUE** can weigh **as much as a whole elephant.** #0254

Its **tail** is **26 ft wide** — almost as long as the world long jump record. #0255

8 FACTS ABOUT OCTOPUSES

The name "octopus" means **"eight feet"** in Greek.
#0256

An octopus has **three hearts.**
#0257

Octopuses swim by **squirting jets of water** behind them. This propels them forward.
#0258

The **female octopus** does not eat while she guards her eggs. She takes care of them for several weeks until they hatch, then **dies of exhaustion.**
#0259

Octopuses have big brains, and can work out how to **unscrew containers.**
#0260

Each octopus arm contains about **50 million brain cells.** The arms do their own thinking.
#0261

When threatened, octopuses squirt **black ink** at their enemies.
#0262

Octopuses have soft bodies, and can squeeze through tiny gaps **less than an inch wide.**
#0263

5 facts about the COLORFUL CUTTLEFISH

A cuttlefish's eyes have "W"-shaped pupils. #0264

A cuttlefish can look to the front or behind without moving its head. #0265

Cuttlefish can change the color of their skin to any pattern they want in less than a second. #0266

Although it can change into any color, a cuttlefish is probably color-blind. #0267

Cuttlefish have green blood. #0268

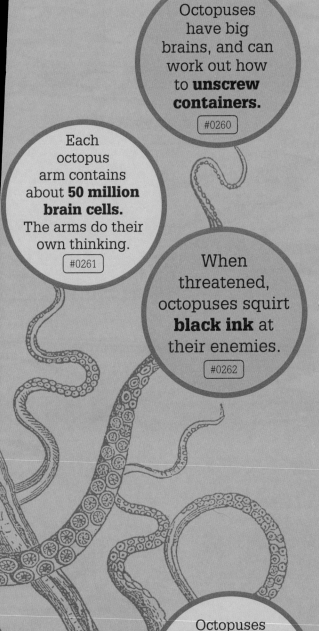

3 FACTS ABOUT
CRABS AND LOBSTERS

LOBSTERS can live for at least **60 years,** and may live for up to **100 years.**

#0269

As they grow, crabs and lobsters **molt their old shells and grow new ones.** #0270

The red crab only lives on Christmas Island in the Indian Ocean, but there are

120 MILLION

of them there. #0271

4 facts about the
HERMIT CRAB

Hermit crabs have **soft bodies,** and climb into empty shells for **protection.**
#0272

The shape of their body changes to fit their shell. #0273

Hermit crabs will **fight each other** for the best shells. #0274

As it grows, a hermit crab must find itself a larger shell. #0275

65

5 FACTS ABOUT JELLYFISH

Jellyfish don't have **BRAINS.**

#0276

Jellyfish do not have **gills.** They **absorb oxygen** through their **thin skin.**

#0277

In 2007, all the fish in a salmon farm off the coast of Northern Ireland were killed by a pack of **billions** of mauve stinger jellyfish.

#0278

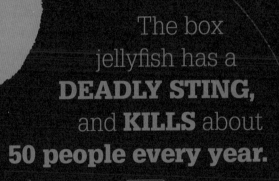

The box
jellyfish has a
DEADLY STING,
and **KILLS** about
50 people every year.

#0279

A human's body is
60 percent water, but a

jellyfish's

body is
more than **90** percent
water.

#0280

67

14 facts about CORAL REEFS
and the fish that live in them

Coral looks like a plant, but is actually a simple kind of animal.
#0281

Reefs build up over time from the hard skeletons of dead coral.
#0282

Reefs grow a few inches each year. Some of the largest began growing **50 million years ago.**
#0283

Reefs get their vivid colors not from the coral, but from the algae that live with them. #0284

Coral likes water that is **79–80°F.** If the water is warmer than this, the coral dies. Global warming is a danger to many reefs. #0285

Coral Reef Creatures

When threatened, a pufferfish will fill itself with water, and balloon up to several times its normal size. #0286

When a starfish loses one of its arms, it grows a new one. #0287

After mating, the male seahorse carries the eggs in a special pouch until they are ready to hatch. #0288

Clownfish live alongside anemones in coral reefs. The anemone provides the fish with food, while the fish protects the anemone from predators. #0289

Coral is very sensitive to pollution. Dirty water kills it. #0290

The Great Barrier Reef

It is the largest coral reef system in the world. It is 1,430 mi long—two-thirds of the distance from New York to Los Angeles. #0291

It contains 2,900 individual reefs. #0292

It also contains more than 900 islands. #0293

It is so big, it can be seen from space. #0294

5 FACTS ABOUT THE

FASTEST FISH

The **sailfish** is the fastest animal in the sea, reaching speeds of

70 mph
—as fast as a car on the freeway. #0295

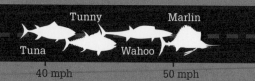

Tuna   Tunny   Wahoo   Marlin

Sailfish

40 mph   50 mph   60 mph   65 mph   70 mph

Second-fastest is the **marlin** at 50 mph. #0296
Third is the **wahoo** at 48 mph. #0297
Fourth is the **tunny** at 46 mph. #0298
Fifth is the **bluefin tuna** at 40 mph. #0299

3 BLUEFIN TUNA FACTS

A bluefin tuna can **weigh** more than **1,100** lb— that's as **heavy** as a horse. #0300

Unusually for fish, the bluefin tuna is **WARM-BLOODED.** #0301

When they are swimming at full SPEED, tuna pull their fins tight to their sides to stay streamlined. #0302

12 FACTS ABOUT
ZOOPLANKTON

Most zooplankton are **small marine animals** that cannot swim. They drift in the ocean currents, **feeding on tiny plants.** #0303

There are more than

14,000

species of **copepod,** tiny crustaceans about **1/16 in** wide.

#0304

The smallest zooplankton are just **2 millionths of a yard** wide.

#0305

Copepods are found wherever there is water, including ditches and damp soil.

#0306

Zooplankton can drift **thousands of miles** ....

Krill start life as drifting zooplankton, before they develop the ability to swim.
#0308

Adult krill often eat their own young.
#0309

The total weight of the **KRILL** in the Antarctic Ocean is greater than the weight of all human beings—it may be more than

500 MILLION TONS.
#0310

Without krill, most life in the Antarctic would DIE!
#0311

Whales travel **thousands of miles** to the polar regions in summer to feed on krill.
#0312

Krill eggs sink to depths of more than 650 ft **before hatching**, to keep them safe from predators.
#0313

Although they are only tiny, **krill can live for up to 10 years.**
#0314

across the ocean in their lifetimes.
#0307

73

10 facts about
SCHOOLING FISH

Cod can grow to **6 ft long—as long as a tall man.** #0315

The largest cod are **200 lb** in weight. #0316

The whiskerlike barbel on a cod's chin helps it to find food on the ocean floor. #0317

A female cod may lay up to **9 million eggs in one go.** #0318

Fish that swim together
are called a school
or a shoal. #0319

Fish of different species
often swim together for
protection. #0320

Atlantic herring form megaschools containing
hundreds of millions
of individuals. #0321

Fish shoal with others of a similar
size and appearance. #0322

Sardines shoal with mackerel,
hake, and anchovy. #0323

Each year, sardine schools swim up the coast of
East Africa, closely followed by predators such as
dolphins, whales, and sharks. These hunters travel long
distances every year to join in the feast. #0324

8 EEL FACTS

The electric eel isn't a real eel at all. It is a kind of fish called a knifefish. #0325

There are more than

400

different species of eel. #0326

A moray eel ties its body into a knot to anchor itself to one place while it eats. #0327

Moray **eels** can grow up to 10 ft long. #0328

A moray eel must open its mouth in order to breathe—this forces water over its gills. #0329

The **European eel** migrates **3,100 mi** to the Sargasso Sea to spawn.

#0330

Europe

Sargasso Sea

Eel larvae float back to Europe from the Sargasso Sea on ocean currents. #0331

Eels can travel distances of up to 110 yd over wet land, by slithering through grass, and digging through wet sand.

#0332

8 FACTS ABOUT HOW
FISH BREATHE

Fish breathe by absorbing oxygen in the water through their gills. #0333

Very active fish have larger gills to take in more oxygen. #0334

Fish gulp in water through their mouths, and force it out through gill slits. #0335

The gills of a 2-lb mackerel have a surface area of 10 square feet—that's the same size as a beach towel. #0336

78

Sharks have between five and seven gill slits on either side of their heads. #0337

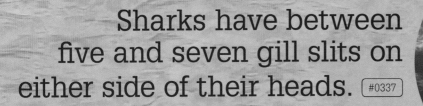

Lungfish have both gills and lungs to breathe. During a dry season when the water dries up, the lungfish survive by burrowing into the mud, and breathing with their lungs. #0338

Mudskippers can breathe through their skin. #0339

They must keep their skin wet at all times in order to breathe. #0340

13 FACTS ABOUT
★ STRANGE ★
SEA
CREATURES

The blobfish's body is mostly made of light jellylike tissue. This helps it to float using very little energy. #0341

The mantis shrimp's eyes are mounted on long stalks. #0342

Young boxfish
have bodies shaped like cubes. #0343

The gurnard takes its name from the "gurr" sound it makes when it is caught. #0344

The male anglerfish is around an inch long. He is dwarfed by the female, which is 8 in long. #0345

The male anglerfish fuses his head to the side of a female, and taps into her bloodstream for food. #0346

The body of the leafy sea dragon is covered in stalks, which make it look like seaweed. #0347

The female jawfish lays eggs, but the male carries them around in his mouth. #0348

GIANTS OF THE SEA

The giant spider crab can grow to 10 ft wide. #0350

The sunflower starfish has up to 40 arms. #0351

Manta rays have wingspans of up to 11½ ft. #0352

The lion's mane jellyfish has a bell-shaped body that is up to 6½ ft wide. #0349

The lion's mane jellyfish's tentacles can reach up to 120 ft—the height of a ten-story building. #0353

10 DEADLY CREATURES

The
STARGAZER FISH
protects itself by giving a sharp **electric shock** to attackers.
#0354

The spines on a **lionfish's** needlelike dorsal fins give a painful sting to predators. #0356

DISGUISED
as a chunk of coral, the reef stonefish kills passing fish with a touch from its venomous spines. #0355

A single **pufferfish** contains enough **poison** to kill

30

people. #0357

The toxic saliva of the blue-ringed octopus can kill a human being in minutes.
#0358

The **banded sea krait**

is a sea snake that has venom

ten times more toxic

than a **rattlesnake's.** #0359

 82

Nudibranches, or sea slugs, are brightly colored. This is a warning that they are **poisonous** to eat. #0360

The **STINGRAY** **uses its venomous tail spines to protect it** from sharks and killer whales. #0361

The **Caribbean fire coral** gets its name from the burning sensation its stinging polyps produce when you touch them. #0362

THE ELECTRIC EEL can produce an electric shock of up to 500 volts—the equivalent of 40 car batteries. #0363

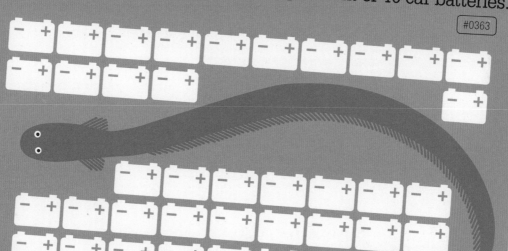

6 FACTS ABOUT flatfish

Flatfish start out life with **eyes** on either side of their **head.** As they grow, one eye **moves over** to the same side as the other. #0364

Flatfish **camouflage** themselves by changing the color and pattern of their skin to match the ocean floor. #0365

The **halibut** is the largest flatfish, growing up to **13 ft long.** #0366

Halibut can live for up to **50 years.** #0367

A tonguefish's eyes are on the **LEFT SIDE** of its body. It lies on its **RIGHT SIDE.** #0369

A YELLOWFIN SOLE'S
eyes are on the right side of its body. It lies on its left side. #0368

4 facts about **HAGFISH**

The Pacific hagfish protects itself by coating its body in **sticky slime.**
#0370

The hagfish is the only known animal that has a **skull** but no backbone.
#0371

Scientists believe that hagfish are closely related to the **earliest fish** that lived more than **400 million years ago.**
#0372

The hagfish has **no jaws,** jut out its teeth to grab prey.
#0373

LIFE IN THE SEA
FACTFILE

INCREDIBLE OCEAN

For the first **3 BILLION** years of life on **EARTH**, living things were only found in the oceans. #0374

We have only explored **1 PERCENT** of the ocean floor. Many more species of marine animal wait to be discovered. #0375

We know more about the **SURFACE OF MARS** than we do about the **ocean floor.** #0376

The **oceans** cover **71 percent** of the planet. #0377

REPRODUCTION

SALMON return from the ocean to the river they were born in to spawn. #0378

Many fish will change sex during their lives.

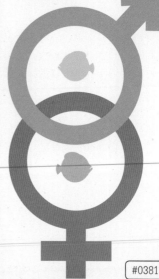

FISH LAY THEIR EGGS in the Sargasso Sea because the dense seaweed protects their young from predators such as **tuna** or **seabirds.** #0379

Sea squirts can **REPRODUCE** by budding. The young **grow out** of the side of the adult's body. #0380

#0381

MARINE **BODIES**

A giant squid's eyes are **12 in across**—the size of a dinner plate. #0382

When threatened, a sea cucumber may **squirt** out some of its internal organs from its bottom. It later **regrows its missing body parts.** #0383

Sea turtles have **special glands** that remove salt from the seawater they drink. #0384

A manatee has **whiskers** that it uses like cutlery, to grasp and take in food. #0385

SOME STARFISH eject their stomachs to cover and digest prey before pulling it back in. #0386

The mantis shrimp has the best eyesight of any animal. Its eyes have **eight different kinds of color sensor,** compared to three in the human eye. #0387

WEIRD BUT TRUE

A lobster's teeth are in its stomach. #0388

SPONGES have the simplest body structure of any animal. #0390

The **Pompeii worm** lives around hot vents on the ocean floor. It can survive in temperatures **up to 175°F.** #0389

The **right whale** #0391 was given its name by whalers because it is slow-moving and easy to hunt.

The **deepest** fish ever found was a cusk eel, which was dredged from the bottom of the Puerto Rico Trench 27,454 ft down. #0392

Sailors once thought that the 50-ft-long oarfish was a man-eating sea monster. #0393

BUGS &
CREEPY CRAWLIES

A QUEEN TERMITE

lays
up to **30,000**
eggs **per day.**

#0394

12 FACTS ABOUT BEETLES

About one third of all animal species are beetles—more than

350,000

and counting. #0395

Beetles have poor eyesight, and mostly communicate using smells. #0396

Stag beetles take their name from their huge jaws, which look like a stag's antlers. #0397

Beetles are found on every continent on Earth. #0398

The fringed ant beetle is the smallest known beetle. It grows to just 1/64 in in length, and weighs 0.14 oz. #0399

Fireflies are a kind of beetle that glows in the dark to attract mates. #0400

The longest beetle is the *Titanus giganteus,* at 6¾ in long. #0401

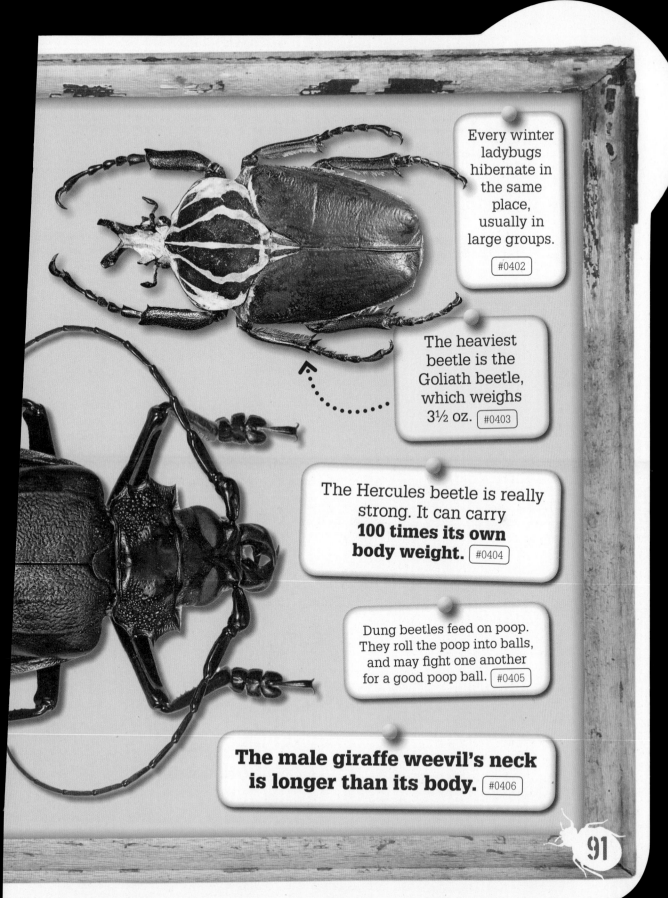

Every winter ladybugs hibernate in the same place, usually in large groups. #0402

The heaviest beetle is the Goliath beetle, which weighs 3½ oz. #0403

The Hercules beetle is really strong. It can carry **100 times its own body weight.** #0404

Dung beetles feed on poop. They roll the poop into balls, and may fight one another for a good poop ball. #0405

The male giraffe weevil's neck is longer than its body. #0406

12 FACTS ABOUT SPINDLY SPIDERS

Spiders have **HUGE BRAINS** for their size. The brains of some spiders even spill over into their legs. #0407

When they are finished with their webs, spiders **eat the silk** to recycle it. #0408

Most spiders have **8 eyes.** #0409

Spider silk shrinks when it gets wet. This means that webs built at dawn are pulled tight by the morning dew. #0410

Spiderlings fly on the wind by making **"kites"** out of silk. #0411

Wolf spider mothers **CARRY THEIR YOUNG** on their backs for several weeks after they are born. #0412

Female nursery web spiders often eat the males after mating with them. #0414

Tarantulas can live for up to 30 YEARS. #0413

The **CRAB SPIDER** can **CHANGE COLOR** to match its surroundings. It hides in wait for unsuspecting prey. #0415

The **largest spiderweb ever found** covered a line of trees **197 YD** long in **Texas.** #0416

The largest spider in the world is the

GOLIATH BIRDEATER

TARANTULA

with a leg span of

12 IN. #0417

Despite its name, the **Goliath birdeater** does not normally feed on birds, but it has been known to take **small hummingbirds.** #0418

93

15 FACTS ABOUT
BUTTERFLIES
and moths

The **largest butterfly** in the world is the **Queen Alexandra's birdwing butterfly**, with a body length of **3¼ in.** #0419

The **painted lady butterfly** is found in more places **around the world** than any other butterfly. #0420

FEMALE BUTTERFLIES have taste receptors in their feet. They drum leaves with their feet to see if they are a good place to lay eggs. #0421

Moths and butterflies **suck up liquid nectar** using their **proboscis** (long, flexible snout). The proboscis of the Morgan's sphinx moth can be over **12 in long.** #0422

Every fall, monarch butterflies migrate from Canada to Mexico, a distance of

1,850 MI.
#0423

Butterflies fly at up to **6 mph.** #0424

The **hawk moth** is the **world's fastest moth,** reaching speeds of more than

30 MPH.
#0425

Cloth moths eat natural fibers in clothes.
#0426

The **largest moth** in the world is the **atlas moth,** with a wingspan of

10 IN.
#0427

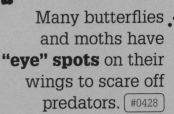

Many butterflies and moths have **"eye" spots** on their wings to scare off predators. #0428

Moths can produce as many as **10 broods** (sets of young) per year. #0429

The brimstone butterfly has the longest lifespan of an adult butterfly: **10 months.** #0430

The adult luna moth has no mouth. It lives for only **1 WEEK,** in which time it does not eat. #0431

Butterflies cannot fly **if they're cold.** #0432

There are about **24,000** species of **butterfly,** and about **140,000** species of **moth.**
#0433

12 ANT
FACTS

The total weight of all the ants in the world is **greater than the weight of all humans.** #0434

There are more than **12,000** different species of ant. #0435

An ant can carry more than **50 times** its own body weight: equivalent to a human lifting a small truck. #0436

Queen ants may live as long as 30 years. #0437

The Maricopa harvester ant is the most venomous insect in the world, with a sting equivalent to that of **12 honeybees.** #0438

Worker, soldier, and queen ants are all female. Male ants have just one job: to mate. #0439

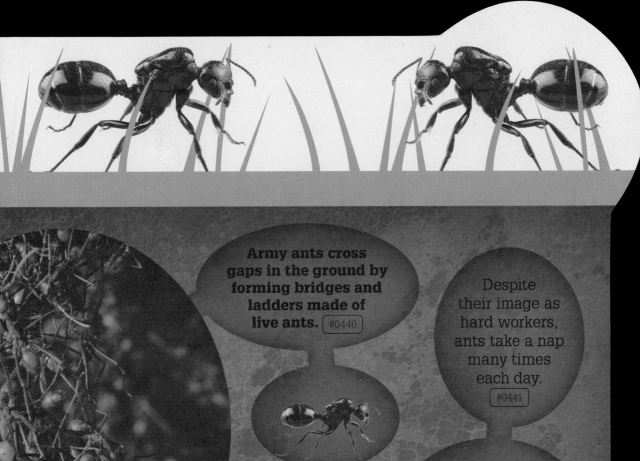

Army ants cross gaps in the ground by forming bridges and ladders made of live ants. #0440

Despite their image as hard workers, ants take a nap many times each day. #0441

An ant has been found perfectly preserved in amber (fossilized tree resin) dating back 92 million years. #0442

In Thailand, weaver ants' eggs are eaten with salad. #0443

In Mexico, ant eggs harvested from the agave plant are considered such a delicacy that they sell for up to $43 per pound. #0444

In Colombia, ants are toasted before being eaten. #0445

97

8 FACTS ABOUT
TERMITES

Termites make mounds above the ground. One in Africa was found to be **42 ft high,** as tall as a two-story building. #0447

Special termites with wings leave their colony to fly off and start new colonies. #0448

Termites feed on a special fungus that only grows in termite mounds. #0450

Termites first appeared on Earth about **250 million years ago**—that's 20 million years before the first dinosaurs. #0446

Termites can't digest their own food. Microscopic bacteria and protozoa in their guts do that job for them. #0449

Soldier termites have such huge jaws that they cannot feed themselves. They are fed by worker termites. #0452

When the mound is attacked, soldier termites protect any holes while the workers repair them from the inside. This leaves the soldiers outside the mound, where they die. #0453

Worker termites walk up to 110 yd search for food for their colony. That is like humans walking 4½ mi to pick up their lunch. #0451

13 **Bee** FACTS

Killer bees will chase you for hundreds of yards if they are threatened.
#0454

Worker bees are all sterile females— they cannot reproduce.
#0455

The honeybee stores the nectar it collects from flowers in pouches behind its legs.
#0456

The honeybee's wings beat about 11,400 times per minute, making its distinctive buzz.
#0457

Honeybees' stingers have a barb that sticks in the victim's body. The bee **leaves its stinger and venom behind, and dies soon afterward.**
#0458

Honeybees visit between **50 and 100** flowers during one trip.
#0459

100

The queen is fertilized by male drone bees. Males do no work at all, and have no sting; all they do is mate.

#0460

The queen bee can lay her own weight in eggs in one day, and up to 200,000 eggs a year.

#0461

The queen bee may mate with up to 17 drones over a 1–2 day period of mating flights.

#0462

Bees build a honeycomb in their nests to house their larvae and stores of honey and pollen.

#0463

Bees "crowd" an intruder to the hive in a ball of bees, raising the temperature around the intruder and killing it.

#0464

During winter, honeybees feed on the honey they made during the summer. They form a tight cluster in their hive to keep the queen and themselves warm.

#0466

The cells of a honeycomb are hexagonal (six-sided) in shape, and made of a fatty substance called beeswax.

#0465

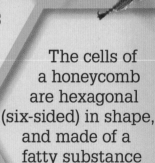

8 FACTS ABOUT  WASPS

Only female wasps have
STINGERS.
Unlike bees, they can sting
more than once. #0467

The **more brightly** colored wasps are usually the ones with the **most painful** sting.

#0468

Paper wasps lay their eggs in nests built from a papery substance made from fibers of dead wood **mixed with saliva.**

#0469

There are more than

30,000

species of wasp.

#0470

Most species of wasp are solitary wasps that live alone. About

1,000

species of wasp are social wasps that live in colonies.

#0471

Female

POTTER WASPS

build urn-shaped mud containers to rear their young.

#0472

When a social wasp dies, it gives off a **special smell** that tells other wasps there is danger around. Nearby wasps are likely to attack when they detect this smell. #0473

Common wasps live in **underground** nests of up to 10,000 individuals. #0474

10 SCORPION FACTS

The **giant desert hairy scorpion** lives in North America. Its body is covered in brown hairs, and it grows up to **5½ IN LONG**.
#0475

Like spiders, **scorpions are arachnids** and have **8 LEGS.**
#0476

Scorpions can live in **extreme conditions.** Some scorpions can survive a night spent in a freezer.
#0477

Some scorpions can slow their bodies down, and survive on just **one meal** a year.
#0478

Before mating, male and female scorpions **clasp each other's pincers and** perform a **ritual dance.**
#0479

Scorpions are found on every continent, except Antarctica.
#0480

WHIP SCORPIONS are not true scorpions as they have **no sting.** They kill their prey by **crushing it** between special teeth on the insides of their front legs.
#0481

All scorpions have a **VENOMOUS sting in their tails.**
#0482

A female scorpion carries her young **on her back** for the first few weeks of their lives while their **skeletons harden.** `#0483`

There are nearly 2,000 species of scorpion, of which about

25 ARE DEADLY TO HUMANS. `#0484`

105

11 BLOOD SUCKER FACTS

Head lice are tiny wingless insects that only **live in human hair.** #0485

The eggs of the head louse are called nits. The female attaches each nit to an individual hair using a special glue that she produces in her body. #0486

A female louse can lay up to 100 nits in 30 days. #0487

The common cat flea can jump 200 times its own length. That's like a human jumping over 325 yd. #0488

Cat fleas prefer to live on cats, but will live on humans if they have to. #0489

Leeches are segmented worms that live in water and suck the blood of other animals. #0490

A leech uses an anesthetic when attaching itself to a host so that the host does not feel it bite. #0491

#0492

A leech will eat up to five times its own body weight.

These ticks have been picked off a koala. The swollen tick has been feeding for two days, and contains a teaspoon of blood. #0493

A tick is a bloodsucking arachnid. It climbs to the end of a branch or leaf, and attaches itself to a host that brushes past. #0494

The chalcid wasp lays its eggs in the bodies of live ticks. The hatching wasps eat their hosts alive. #0495

107

7 MOSQUITO facts

A mosquito's wings beat **500 times per second.** #0496

Before mating, male and female mosquitoes synchronize their wingbeats so that they are flying at the same speed. #0497

Male mosquitoes feed on plant sap and nectar. Only the females bite and suck blood. #0498

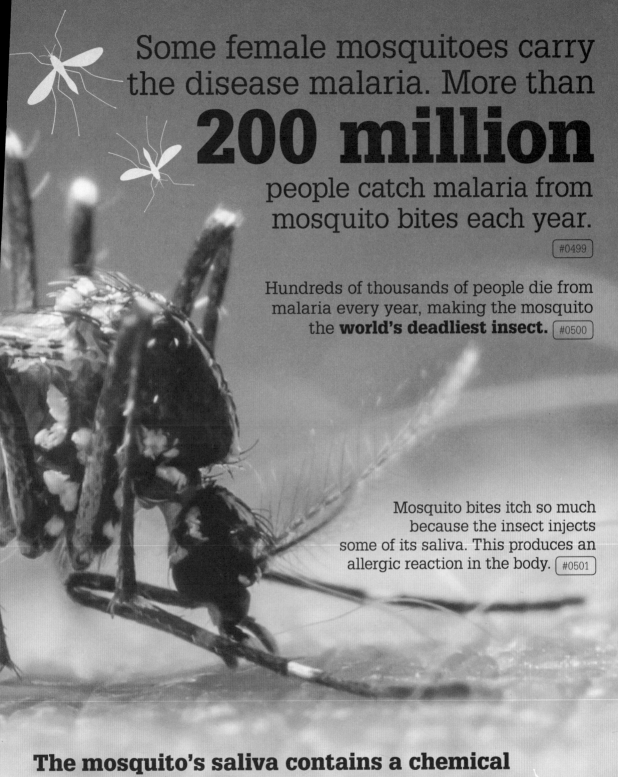

Some female mosquitoes carry the disease malaria. More than **200 million** people catch malaria from mosquito bites each year. #0499

Hundreds of thousands of people die from malaria every year, making the mosquito the **world's deadliest insect.** #0500

Mosquito bites itch so much because the insect injects some of its saliva. This produces an allergic reaction in the body. #0501

The mosquito's saliva contains a chemical that keeps blood from clotting, so that it carries on flowing as she feeds. #0502

109

10 FACTS ABOUT
FLIES

Fruit flies live for 8–10 days as adults. In that time, a female lays around 500 eggs in rotting fruit or vegetables. The eggs hatch into maggots. #0503

The robber fly chases and seizes other insects in the air. It catches its prey in its long, spiny legs, and sucks out the insides with its sharp proboscis. #0504

Female horseflies suck blood from horses and other animals, including humans. #0505

Flies can smell meat up to
4½ mi away.

#0506

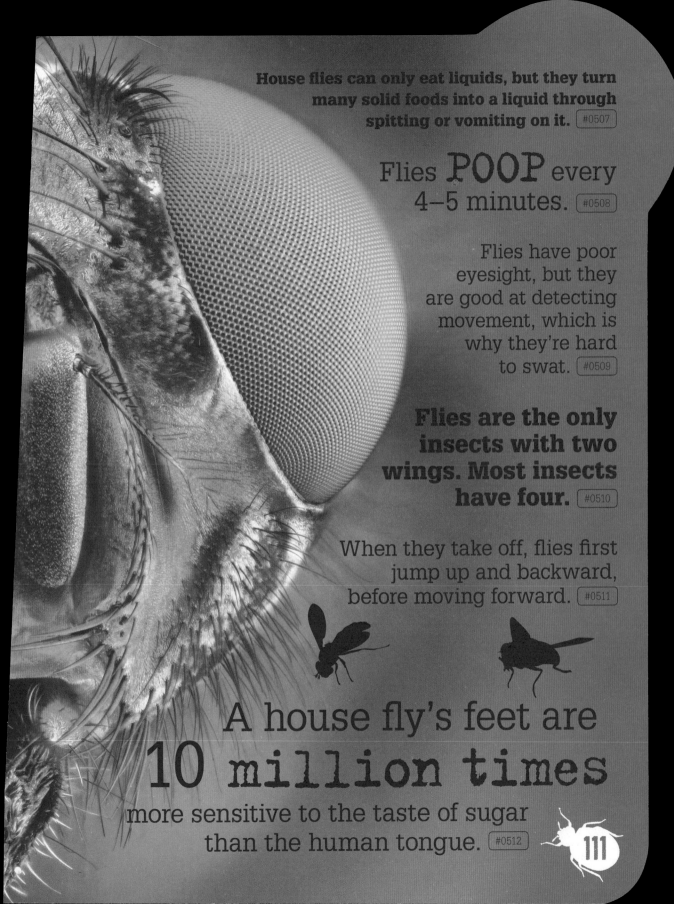

House flies can only eat liquids, but they turn many solid foods into a liquid through spitting or vomiting on it. #0507

Flies POOP every 4–5 minutes. #0508

Flies have poor eyesight, but they are good at detecting movement, which is why they're hard to swat. #0509

Flies are the only insects with two wings. Most insects have four. #0510

When they take off, flies first jump up and backward, before moving forward. #0511

A house fly's feet are 10 million times more sensitive to the taste of sugar than the human tongue. #0512

111

7 FACTS ABOUT THE
UNBREAKABLE
'ROACH

Cockroaches can live for weeks without their **HEADS.**

#0513

There are about **4,000** different species of cockroach, but **only about 30 are considered pests.**

#0514

Some **female cockroaches** incubate their eggs in a sac attached to their bodies.

#0515

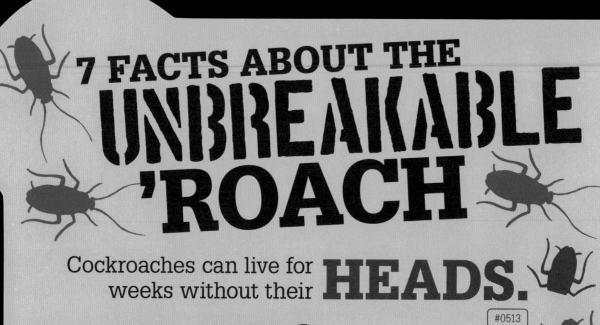

When alarmed, the **Madagascar hissing cockroach** makes a hissing sound **through breathing holes in its abdomen.**

#0516

The largest **cockroach** MEGALOBLATTA LONGIPENNIS has a wingspan of **7 in.** #0517

Cockroaches can **eat just about anything,** including glue, paper, grease, soap, leather, and even hair. They can **survive for long periods** without any food at all. #0518

Cockroaches are *FAST* moving at up to

30 IN

per second. They can detect approaching threats by sensing changes in air currents. #0519

8 FACTS ABOUT
GRASSHOPPERS
AND LOCUSTS

As well as jumping, grasshoppers are also **strong flyers.** #0520

Grasshoppers make music by rubbing their hind legs against their forewings. #0521

Grasshoppers' ears are on their bellies (on each side of the abdominal segment). #0522

LOCUSTS are grasshoppers that have come together into **giant swarms.** Swarms of locusts can destroy CROPS. #0523

A locust can eat the equivalent of its **own body weight** in one day.
#0524

Grasshoppers are edible, and a very good source of protein. #0525

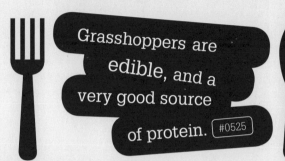

The largest recorded

SWARM

of locusts occurred in 1875 in the U.S. It was 1,860 mi long and 112 mi wide, and contained trillions of insects. Thousands of farms were destroyed.
#0526

A grasshopper can **jump** up to **20 times** its own body length. #0527

5 MANTID FACTS

Mantids have the largest claws of any insects. #0528

Mantids catch other insects with their claws, but also prey on small frogs, lizards, and mice. #0529

Different species of flower mantis are colored to match the particular flowers they perch on. #0530

The hooded mantid's body is shaped like two leaves so it can hide on plants. #0531

The female mantid is much larger than the male. She eats him after they have mated. #0532

Vs 3 DRAGONFLY FACTS

Dragonflies are fierce predators. They eat flies, bees, ants, and wasps. #0533

Dragonflies can reach speeds of over 30 mph— that's faster than an Olympic sprinter. #0534

A dragonfly's huge eyes give it almost 360-degree vision. #0535

3 FACTS ABOUT INSECTS

THAT LIVE INSIDE OTHER INSECTS

Some insects live inside other insects, **often killing them.** These are known as **parasitoid insects.** #0536

The **SMALLEST INSECT** is the fairyfly. The males are just 0.006 in long. The females lay their eggs inside the eggs of other insects. #0537

The *Clemelis pullata* fly lays eggs so small that they are **swallowed whole** by caterpillars. The eggs hatch in the caterpillar's stomach, and the hatchlings **eat the caterpillar alive.** #0538

3 BEDBUG facts

There are 92

different species of bedbug. #0539

Bedbugs can survive for months without food, lying in wait for someone to bite. #0540

Bedbugs are bloodsucking insects that live in **cracks** and crevices **in and around our beds.** #0541

119

9 Caterpillar
facts

A caterpillar's first meal is the shell of its egg. #0542

Caterpillars spend their whole time eating, increasing their body weight by up to 1,000 times in just a few weeks. #0543

Some caterpillars are brightly colored as a warning to birds or other predators that they are poisonous to eat. #0544

The walnut sphinx moth caterpillar makes a high-pitched whistle to scare off birds. #0545

Caterpillars may change color as they grow. #0546

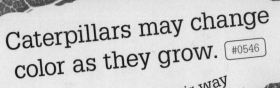

Buff-tip caterpillars eat their way through leaves in teams. #0547

Caterpillars have six eyes on either side of their heads, but they have very poor eyesight. #0548

When they are ready to turn into adults, caterpillars spin themselves a silk cocoon to make a pupa. They emerge a few weeks, months, or even years later as adults, known as imagos. #0549

embryo

larva

Butterflies and moths have four life stages: embryo, larva, pupa, and imago. #0550

pupa

imago

BUGS & CREEPY CRAWLIES

FACTFILE

FRIENDS AND **PESTS**

ANTS' WORST ENEMIES
are other ants. Ants from other colonies, even of the same species, are treated as enemies to be invaded and destroyed.

#0551

The tiny pharaoh ant is **A MAJOR PEST** in hospitals and offices in tropical countries. It can make a nest between two sheets of paper.

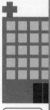

#0552

Aphids are tiny insects that **destroy crops** and garden flowers. They feed by **sucking** the sap from the stems of the plants.

#0553

BEES
are essential to human agriculture.

Their nectar gathering from one flower to another pollinates our crops.

#0554

BUG **BEHAVIOR**

Grasshoppers can **SPIT A BROWN FLUID** when threatened. This was once known as "tobacco juice" because grasshoppers would feed on tobacco crops.

#0555

The rubytail wasp, or cuckoo wasp, lays its

eggs

in the nests of other bees or wasps. When the eggs hatch, the grubs eat the hosts' grubs and food stores.

#0556

Army ants can set up **"camp"** for the night by forming **a large bivouac** made entirely of the ants' bodies.

#0557

Honeybees point other bees in the direction of food by **dancing.**

THE MOVEMENTS

indicate the direction and distance to fly in to find the food.

#0558

YUCKY BUGS

The best way to **remove a leech** is with your **fingernail.** Never use a flame to remove a leech. It will **vomit its stomach contents** into your wound, and could cause disease.

The larva of the lily beetle protects itself from predators by covering its whole body in its own **runny poop.** #0561

After studying **300,000 flies,** researchers in China concluded that the average house fly carries 2 million bacteria on its body. #0559

#0560

 If a fly **SPOTS** a group of flies, it will join them. That's why sticky flypaper works so well. #0564

Fly maggots feed on **ROTTING FLESH.** #0562

House flies are particularly attracted to **pet poop** because it really **pongs** and is easy for them to find. #0563

WEIRD BUT TRUE

The mantid looks like it is praying when it holds its front legs up. This led the ancient Greeks to think it had supernatural powers. #0565

A scorpion's body glows under **ULTRAVIOLET LIGHT.** #0566

The **LARGEST** ant colony ever found was a colony of Argentinian ants that stretched **3,730 mi** along the Mediterranean coast. #0567

The peppered moth has evolved with its changing human environment. As pollution from factories darkened trees during the 19th century, the moth gradually changed from white to black, **to hide from predators.** #0568

Like adult insects, caterpillars have just **six legs.** The rest of the legs you see are "false legs," which they use to hold on to leaves as they feed.
#0570

CATERPILLAR POOP is called "frass." It contains lots of nutrients for plants, and makes an excellent fertilizer. #0569

CHAPTER 4

LIFE IN THE AIR

FLAMINGOS
can live in a variety
of habitats, even
salt lakes ...

... Special glands
near their beaks
can filter out
excess salt as
they feed. #0571

5 Beautiful **bird** facts

In many species of bird, **only the male has COLORFUL FEATHERS.** #0572

The male greater bird of paradise

FANS OUT HIS WINGS

and puffs up his tail feathers in a display to the females. #0573

The peacock fans his tail feathers to **ATTRACT MATES.** The tail feathers can **GROW TO MORE THAN 3 FT LONG.** They fall out and regrow each year. #0574

Malachite kingfishers **bash the heads of fish** they have caught against tree trunks to **kill** them. #0575

Both the male and the female scarlet macaw have brilliant red, yellow, and blue feathers. However, males don't have to impress new females each year as these birds **mate for life.** #0576

127

12 **Hummingbird** FACTS

Hummingbirds are the only birds that can fly **backward.** #0577

Hummingbirds hover in front of flowers to feed on nectar. They have long beaks to reach right inside the flower. #0578

Hummingbirds can even fly **upside down.** #0579

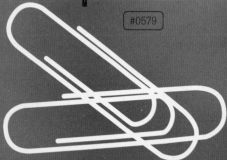

A hummingbird's wings flap between **12 and 100** times a second, producing the

that gives the bird its name. #0580

The bee hummingbird is the smallest bird in the world. It weighs **just 0.07 oz**—about the weight of two paperclips. #0581

The vervain hummingbird's egg is **3/8 in long** and weighs just 0.01 oz. #0582

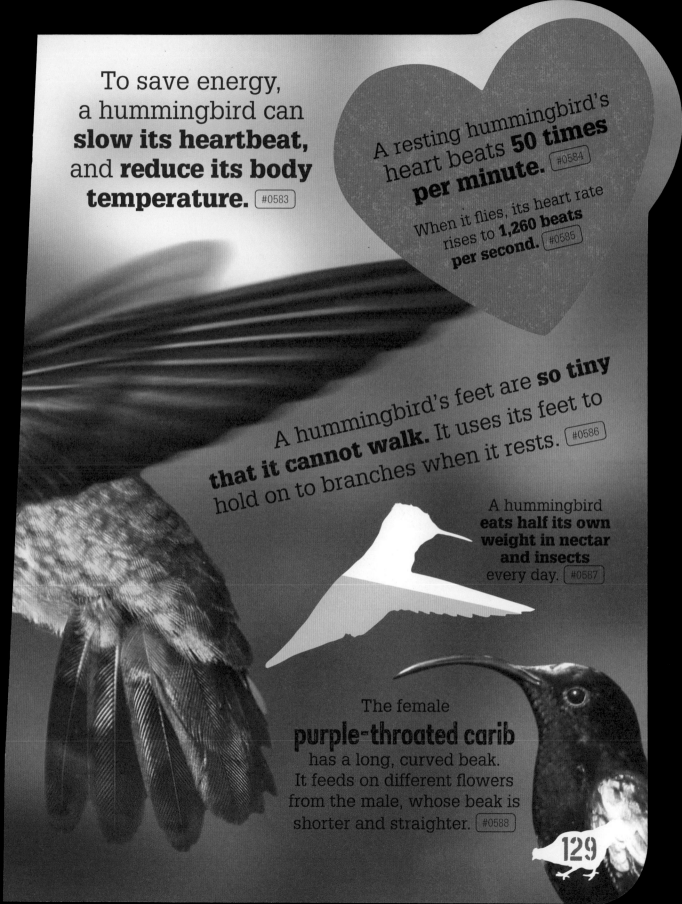

To save energy, a hummingbird can **slow its heartbeat,** and **reduce its body temperature.** #0583

A resting hummingbird's heart beats **50 times per minute.** #0584 When it flies, its heart rate rises to **1,260 beats per second.** #0585

A hummingbird's feet are **so tiny that it cannot walk.** It uses its feet to hold on to branches when it rests. #0586

A hummingbird **eats half its own weight in nectar and insects** every day. #0587

The female **purple-throated carib** has a long, curved beak. It feeds on different flowers from the male, whose beak is shorter and straighter. #0588

129

5 FACTS ABOUT BIG-BRAINED BIRDS

New Caledonian crows **use twigs and trimmed leaves as tools** to get at food in hard-to-reach nooks.

#0589

Crows can recognize **HUMAN FACES.** They will **attack** people who have previously attacked them or a crow they know.

#0590

In Japan, crows have learned to drop nuts at pedestrian crossings. Passing cars **crush the shells,** and the crows **wait for the green light** to walk out and eat them in safety. #0591

MIGRATING CROWS will change their route to avoid a place where crows have previously been shot. #0592

Scrub jays

will pretend to **hide their food** if they know other scrub jays are watching, but they will really be taking it somewhere else. #0593

4 FACTS ABOUT A TALKING PARROT

An African gray parrot called **ALEX** was taught a vocabulary of more than **100 WORDS.** #0594

Alex could **IDENTIFY** more than 50 different objects, **COUNT** up to six, and **DISTINGUISH** between seven different **COLORS.** #0595

Scientists think Alex displayed **an ability to think** equivalent to that of a four-year-old child. #0596

When he was tired, Alex would give **WRONG ANSWERS** on purpose to make the test stop—**just like a stroppy child.** #0597

131

8 FACTS ABOUT
Hornbills

The rhinoceros hornbill's casque (crest) curves like the shape of a **rhino's horn.**

#0598

A hornbill's casque acts like a **sound chamber,** to make its calls much louder.

#0599

A hornbill has **EYELASHES MADE FROM MODIFIED FEATHERS,** which shade the eyes from the sun.

#0600

Hornbills can live for up to **70 YEARS.**

#0601

GROUND HORNBILL

pairs need the help of at least **two relatives** to rear their young. Hornbills spend several years helping other birds before they have their own chicks.

#0602

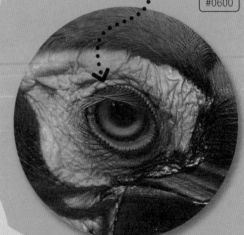

When nesting, female hornbills **wall themselves up inside tree trunks** where they will stay with their chicks **for four months.**

#0603

The chicks stay with their parents for **SIX MONTHS** after leaving the nest.

#0605

While they are inside the nest, the female and her chicks are **fed through a narrow slit in the wall** by the male.

#0604

132

5 FACTS ABOUT TOUCANS

It uses its bill to reach for fruits, **search holes** in tree trunks, and steal food from other birds' nests.
#0606

A toucan's tongue is up to 6 in long.
#0607

Its bill measures half the bird's entire body length.
#0608

A toucan's **HUGE BILL** is **HOLLOW** AND **LIGHT.**
#0609

The bill is **serrated,** which helps it to hold on to **PREY** such as a small lizard.
#0610

5 FACTS ABOUT
BIRDS
OF PREY

Kestrels hover in the air scanning the ground for prey. When they see movement, they dive. #0611

The peregrine falcon is the world's fastest animal. It reaches **186 mph** when it dives. That's as fast as a bullet train. #0612

Bald eagles build huge nests up to **13 ft tall**— taller than **two people** standing on top of each other. #0613

The secretary bird catches its prey by chasing it on the ground. It kills the prey by stamping on it. #0614

The smallest bird of prey is the Asian black-thighed falconet, which is just 6 in long. #0615

5 OWL
FACTS

An owl can turn its head almost all of the way around.
#0616

It needs to turn its head because its eyes cannot move in their sockets. The eyes are very large so that it can see at night. #0617

An owl's wings have special downy feathers that allows it to fly very quietly. This helps them to sneak up on prey at night. #0618

An owl's neck is very flexible because it has 14 bones in it. The human neck has just 7 bones. #0619

Owls are long-sighted, and cannot focus on anything closer than a few inches away. #0620

5 Vulture facts

Vultures use their **powerful hooked beaks** to rip open the tough skin of dead bodies.

#0621

A vulture's head and neck are **bald** or covered in **short feathers**. This allows it to reach deep inside dead bodies as it feeds.

#0622

Vultures have **EXCELLENT EYESIGHT**, and can spot a dying animal on the ground **MANY MILES AWAY.**

#0623

On hot days, vultures **pee on their legs** to cool down. The urine also helps to kill harmful bacteria on their bodies.

#0624

Up to **six different species of vulture** may **FEED ON THE SAME CARCASS,** each tucking into a different part of the body.

#0625

4 FACTS ABOUT **CONDORS**

The Andean condor has the **largest wing surface area of any bird,** at about

775 IN².

#0626

The condor uses its

huge wings

to soar high into the air on rising air currents. It can reach heights of over **13,000 ft.** #0627

The wingspan of the **Andean condor** can be as long as **10½ ft.** Each wing is as long as an average adult woman. #0628

Condors have **ONE CHICK** every other year. It takes them **A WHOLE YEAR** to rear the chick. #0629

4 FACTS ABOUT
COURTING BIRDS

A male barn owl will bring a female **a gift of a dead mouse** in an effort to win her affections. #0630

The male bowerbird is an

artist.

He builds a display using twigs and brightly colored objects to impress the females.

#0631

MALE NIGHTINGALES sing at night to impress the females. At dawn, they sing to defend their territories.

#0632

MALE FRIGATEBIRDS have giant red pouches under their bills, which **INFLATE** to attract a mate.

#0633

④ EGG-CITING FACTS

Wandering albatrosses incubate their eggs for

78 days.

#0634

24 hen's eggs could fit into one ostrich egg.

#0635

Ospreys lay **THREE EGGS,** but the eggs do not hatch at the same time. **THE CHICK THAT HATCHES FIRST** is the one most likely to survive. #0636

The European blue tit lays up to 16 eggs in one clutch. #0637

5 GEESE FACTS

When they migrate, Canada geese fly in a **"V" formation** as this is the most aerodynamic arrangement.

#0638

The birds take turns flying at the **FRONT OF THE "V,"** dropping back when they get tired.

#0639

With the right wind, geese can cover 1,500 mi in **24 HOURS.**

#0640

A flock of 50 geese produces **2.5 tons of poop** in a year, which is heavier than two large cars.

#0641

Canada geese look after their young in **communal creches,** which may contain over 100 goslings.

#0642

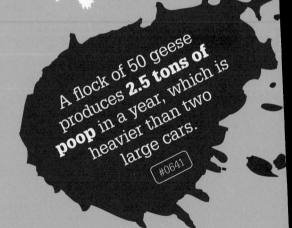

140

7 FACTS ABOUT DUCKS & SWANS

A fear of swans is called **CYGNOPHOBIA.**

#0643

Swans are **highly intelligent,** and can remember **who has been kind to them and who hasn't.** #0644

Swans' beaks have **JAGGED EDGES** to help them catch fish.

#0645

The female mallard lines her nest with downy feathers that she **plucks from her own undercoat.** #0646

A duck covers its outer feathers with OIL made in a gland near its tail. The oil **MAKES THE FEATHERS WATERPROOF.**

#0647

Twice a year, mallards shed their flight feathers. They are unable to fly for several weeks while **new feathers grow.** #0648

Just one day after hatching, **ducklings can run, swim, and forage** for their own food. #0649

6 LONG-DISTANCE FLIGHT FACTS

Alaska,
U.S.

Every fall, the
bar-tailed godwit flies
from Alaska to New
Zealand, a distance of
6,835 mi.

#0650

New
Zealand

The godwit
does this journey in
eight days
and flies nonstop without
a single break. #0651

The birds build up
fat reserves before the
journey, and use these reserves
for energy as they fly. #0652

The Arctic tern flies a
43,500 mi
round trip from the Arctic to Antarctica and back again every year. #0653

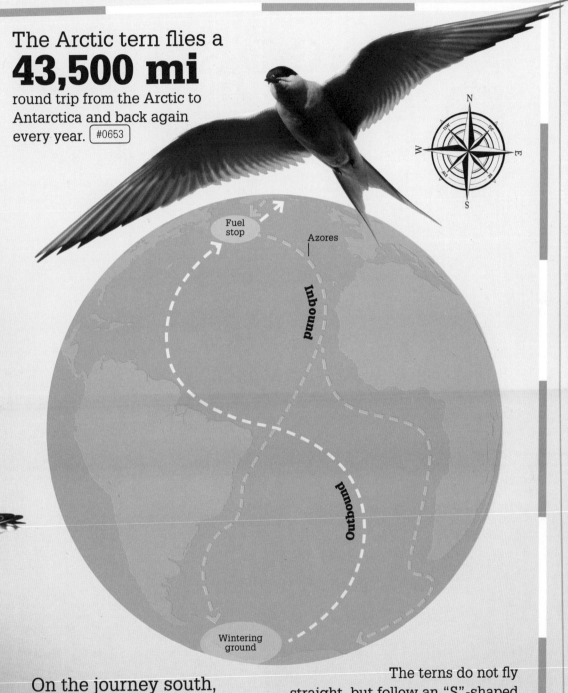

Fuel stop

Azores

Inbound

Outbound

Wintering ground

On the journey south, the birds stop for a while in the Azores to feed. #0654

The terns do not fly straight, but follow an "S"-shaped route. This allows them to take advantage of the prevailing winds. #0655

11 FACTS ABOUT
FLIGHTLESS BIRDS

The giant moa of New Zealand stood nearly **12 ft tall**—twice the height of an adult human. It died out about **500 years ago.** #0656

12 ft

A **female kiwi** lays a single egg in a season. The egg is about **20 percent** of the mother's body weight—the largest egg, proportionally, of any bird. #0657

The kiwi has **NOSTRILS** on the end of its long beak, which it uses to sniff out food in the undergrowth. #0658

On hot days, emus **ROLL AROUND** on their backs in streams to keep cool. #0659

An ostrich
can run at
45 MPH.
#0660

As it runs, an ostrich
uses its wings
to help it to steer.
#0661

It travels up to **16 ft** in one stride.
#0662

An ostrich's
POWERFUL KICK
can kill a human.
#0663

The ostrich has the **largest eye** of any land animal.

It is **2 in** across.

An ostrich's eye is
larger than
its brain.
#0664

#0665

(2 in)

Many **dinosaurs** had the same leg structure as ostriches.

Scientists study the way **ostriches run** to give them an

understanding of how dinosaurs moved. #0666

145

10 PENGUIN

FACTS

Penguins in **Antarctica** are easy to film. They have no predators on land, so they are not afraid of humans. #0667

Most penguins live in cold places, but the **Galápagos penguin** lives near the equator. #0669

Rather than walk, penguins slide down icy hills on their bellies. #0671

All penguins live in the southern hemisphere. #0668

As they swim, penguins leap out of the water in arcs— an action called **porpoising.** #0670

Antarctica

The emperor penguin breeds in the Antarctic winter. The females leave the eggs with the males, who huddle together in their thousands in **temperatures of**

-58°F.

#0673

The males incubate the eggs by **balancing them on their feet for 64 days.**

#0674

By the time the egg hatches, the male has not eaten for **115 days.**

#0676

Emperor penguins can stay underwater for **18 minutes,** and dive to depths of

1,750 ft.

#0672

The emperor penguin stands 4 ft tall, and weighs up to 100 lb. It is the largest species of penguin.

#0675

9 facts about bird
supersenses

IRON-RICH BLOOD CELLS

have been found in the tops of homing pigeons' beaks. These all point north, like needles on a compass. #0677

Homing pigeons

often **follow roads** on the ground as they fly home. They even turn off at junctions.

#0678

Birds can sense the Earth's **magnetic field.** This helps them to **find their way** on long journeys. #0679

During **World War II,** some aircraft carried pigeons on board. Airmen would **send messages home** attached to the pigeons if their planes were shot down. #0680

148

In addition to magnetism, homing pigeons use the position of the Sun to help them navigate.

Observed Sun

Expected Sun

Home Sun at noon

#0681

Eyesight is the **MOST IMPORTANT SENSE** for many birds. Their vision is **TWO TO THREE TIMES** more detailed than human vision.

#0682

Many birds can see **ultraviolet light.** Their bright plumage looks even more colorful to their eyes. #0684

Most birds have a

POOR

sense of **TASTE** and **SMELL.**

#0683

Oilbirds live in dark caves, and use ECHOLOCATION to find their way around. They bounce sounds off objects and listen for the echo. #0685

4 FACTS ABOUT CRAFTY
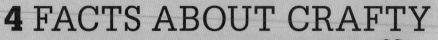
CUCKOOS

Cuckoos lay their eggs in the nests of **other birds.**

#0686

In some species, **THE MALE WILL LURE** the host birds away from their nest while **THE FEMALE** creeps in and lays her egg.

#0687

Usually, the **host birds** do not realize that the cuckoo is not really their chick and **continue to feed it**. Often the host bird is a much smaller bird such as a robin, and it must work extra-hard to feed the hungry cuckoo chick.

#0688

The **cuckoo egg hatches first** and the chick pushes the other eggs out of the nest. #0689

5 facts about **nests**

Red-cockaded woodpeckers excavate **HOLES IN TREE TRUNKS** to make their nests. It takes 2–3 years to build a nest, which they may use for the next 20 years. #0690

Edible-nest

swiftlets make their nests from hardened saliva. The nests are used in Southeast Asia to make bird's nest soup. #0691

The **buff-breasted paradise kingfisher** builds its nest on top of termite mounds. #0692

Weaver birds

weave elaborate nests in trees from twigs and leaves. The entrance is at the bottom of the nest. #0694

Sociable weavers build **HUGE COMMUNAL NESTS** with room for up to 100 pairs inside. #0693

5 RECORD-BREAKING BIRDS

The chicken is the **most common** bird in the world. There are about

50,000,000,000

of them. #0695

Weighing in at up to 40 lb, **male kori bustards** and **great bustards** share the record for the

heaviest

flying birds. #0696

The wandering albatross has the

longest
wingspan

of any bird—up to **11½ ft.** #0697

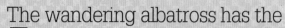

Rüppell's griffon vulture is possibly the

highest flier,

climbing to over **32,000 ft.** #0698

The Australian pelican has the

longest
beak.

It can be up to **18 in long.**

#0699

153

5 FACTS ABOUT
Fishing birds

A wood stork can snap its beak shut around a fish in

25
milliseconds.

#0700

The **American white pelican** can hold **3 gallons** of water in its bill.

#0701

As well as doing their own fishing, **pelicans poach food from other birds,** chasing them until they drop their prey.

#0702

When it lands, a **CORMORANT** will STRETCH **ITS WINGS OUT** to dry them after diving in water.

#0703

Gannets dive
into the sea at speeds of up to 60 mph from heights of up to 100 ft.

#0704

154

5 FACTS ABOUT GULLS

Gulls drop mollusks onto rocks to break them open to eat. #0705

Seagulls are **CARING PARENTS.** Males and females pair for life, and take turns incubating their eggs. #0706

A herring gull chick taps on a red spot on its parents' beaks to get them to **regurgitate their food** for the chick to eat. #0707

Gulls are omnivores, and will **scavenge trash cans** for anything remotely edible. #0708

Gulls **STAMP ON THE GROUND** to imitate rainfall. This **TRICKS WORMS** into coming to the surface. #0709

155

4 STARLING
FACTS

A flock of starlings is called a murmuration. Before they roost for the night, starlings form huge, **ball-shaped murmurations.**

#0710

Each bird tries to match its neighbors' speed and direction.

#0711

The constantly changing shape of the murmuration makes it difficult for birds of prey to attack any of the starlings.

#0712

One murmuration in Goole, England, included
1.5 MILLION BIRDS.

#0713

5 **Sparrow** FACTS

A pair of sparrows will raise two or even three broods in one year. #0715

Sparrows have been known to nest in **coalmines** hundreds of feet underground.
#0716

House sparrows live mainly in urban areas, but may move to the countryside around harvest time.
#0717

Sparrows have lived alongside humans since the Stone Age. #0718

157

LIFE IN THE AIR
FACTFILE

BIRD **BEHAVIOR**

Male superb lyrebirds woo females by raising their 20-in-long tail feathers over their heads. #0719

The male lyrebird also uses song and dance to impress females. #0720

Sparrows often **STEAL OTHER BIRDS' NESTS** rather than building their own. #0721

Honeyguides can lead humans to beehives. When the humans break open the hives for their honey, the bird is usually given some honey as a reward. #0722

WEIRD BUT TRUE

Birds are the only animals alive today that **EVOLVED FROM DINOSAURS.** #0723

A turkey vulture **throws up** when it is threatened. #0724

In 2013, a completely new species of bird, the Cambodian tailorbird, was discovered living in the large city of Phnom Penh, Cambodia. #0725

Scientists have increasing evidence that birds are descended from dinosaurs, and that many dinosaurs were feathered. #0726

A barn owl's heart-shaped face helps it channel sound waves to its ears. #0728

A sparrow's place in the **pecking order** is determined by the **size of its bib** (the colored part of its breast). #0727

BIRD **FEEDING**

A puffin can hold up to **80 SAND EELS** in its beak at a time.

#0731

If a gardener is digging, a robin will follow the gardener in the hope of **PICKING UP WORMS.**

#0729

A wren will feed its young more than **500 spiders** and **caterpillars** in a single day.

#0730

The **Baltimore oriole** can eat up to 17 caterpillars in a minute.

#0732

AMAZING **BIRDS**

THE BIGGEST PARROT SPECIES is the hyacinth macaw, which grows up to

3 FEET IN LENGTH.

#0734

There are about **10,000** species of bird.

#0733

#0735

Cuckoos arriving in Northern Europe in April are often seen as the **START OF SPRING.**

The male cassowary incubates the eggs, and cares for the chicks. The female does little to help.

#0736

THREE MILLION

pairs of Macaroni penguins breed on the island of South Georgia.

#0737

The finches of the Galápagos Islands have differently sized and shaped **beaks** depending on their diet.

#0738

REPTILES

CHAPTER 5

A crocodile's
JAWS
are designed for biting and snapping shut, but the muscles needed to open them are very weak. **So the best way to beat a croc in a fight is to tape its mouth shut!**

#0739

11 LIZARD FACTS

There are about **5,000** **different species** of lizard.
#0740

Lizards smell by sticking out their **tongues.** #0741

In the **BREEDING SEASON**, male agama lizards turn their heads and tails **BRIGHT ORANGE** and their bodies **BLUE** in order to attract females.
#0742

When threatened by a predator, the armadillo girdled lizard **curls up** and becomes an **unappetizing spiky ball.**
#0744

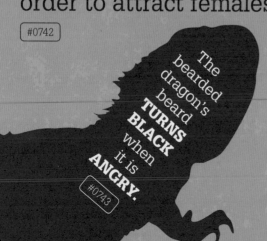

The bearded dragon's beard **TURNS BLACK** when it is **ANGRY.**
#0743

Skinks are lizards with **short necks** and **short legs.** Some have no legs at all, and move like snakes. #0745

Glass lizards look like snakes, but they have the eyelids and ear openings of a lizard. #0746

Caiman lizards eat almost nothing other than **snails.** #0747

Lizards can give a **painful bite,** but none is as venomous as some snakes'. #0748

The **common basilisk** can **run on water,** and is sometimes called the **Jesus Christ lizard.** #0749

Many lizards have a **DEWLAP**, which is a loose flap of skin that grows down under the chin. They use these to **COMMUNICATE WITH EACH OTHER.** #0750

163

4 GILA MONSTER FACTS

A Gila monster spends about 90 percent of its life hiding in its burrow. #0751

The Gila monster is named after the Gila River in Arizona, where it lives, and has a thick, forked tongue that makes snorting hisses. #0752

It kills its prey with a venomous bite. The venom is extremely painful to a human, but not strong enough to kill. #0753

A Gila monster's sense of smell is so keen it can sniff out a buried bird's egg to eat, or follow a trail made by a rolling egg. #0754

4 KOMODO DRAGON FACTS

The Komodo dragon is the **largest lizard in the world,** growing up to 10 ft long. #0755

It can sense prey from up to 5 mi away **using its tongue!** #0756

It preys on large mammals, including horses and deer. #0757

The muscles in its jaws and throat allow it to swallow huge chunks of meat very quickly. #0758

7 FACTS ABOUT
WORM LIZARDS

Most worm lizards have **no arms or legs,** and spend all their lives under soil. #0759

They use their heads to dig tunnels through the ground. #0760

The **MEXICAN** MOLE LIZARD is a type of worm lizard that has **tiny forearms,** which it uses to dig. It has **no rear legs.** #0761

Worm lizards can move **BACKWARD** just as easily as they move **FORWARD.** #0762

They move like an

ACCORDION,

rippling their loose skin to pull themselves forward. #0763

166

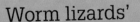

Worm lizards'
eyes and ears are
covered by skin,
giving them **poor HEARING and VISION.**

#0764

Some species of worm lizard keep
their eggs in their bodies and
give birth
to live
young.

#0765

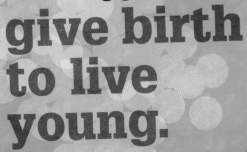

10 FACTS ABOUT GECKOS

The eyes of a gecko are **350** times more **SENSITIVE TO LIGHT** than human eyes.
#0766

Most geckos **HUNT AT NIGHT.**
#0767

A gecko can hold its **whole body weight** on one toe. #0768

Geckos shed their skin every two to four weeks, then eat it. #0769

Most geckos **CLING** to smooth vertical surfaces **USING MILLIONS OF TINY HAIRS** on their feet.
#0770

Leopard geckos have claws instead of **sticky pads.** #0771 ·······→

The flying gecko cannot actually fly. It glides using **skin flaps** connected to its feet. #0772

If attacked, a gecko can **BREAK OFF ITS TAIL,** escape, and then grow another. #0773

Most geckos have fixed eyelids and **CANNOT BLINK.** #0774

Like all lizards, geckos are **COLD-BLOODED.** They must lie in the sun all day to make them warm enough to hunt through the night. #0775

169

DESERT LIZARDS

The horny toad has the **ROUNDED BODY** of a toad, but it is actually a lizard. It is also known as the **HORNED LIZARD.** #0776

 To scare off predators, horned lizards **squirt blood** from the corners of their eyes. #0777

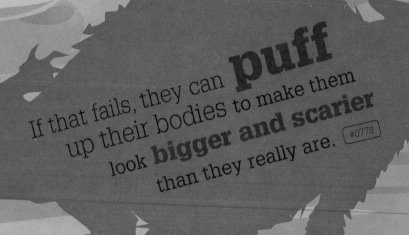

If that fails, they can **puff** up their bodies to make them look **bigger and scarier** than they really are. #0778

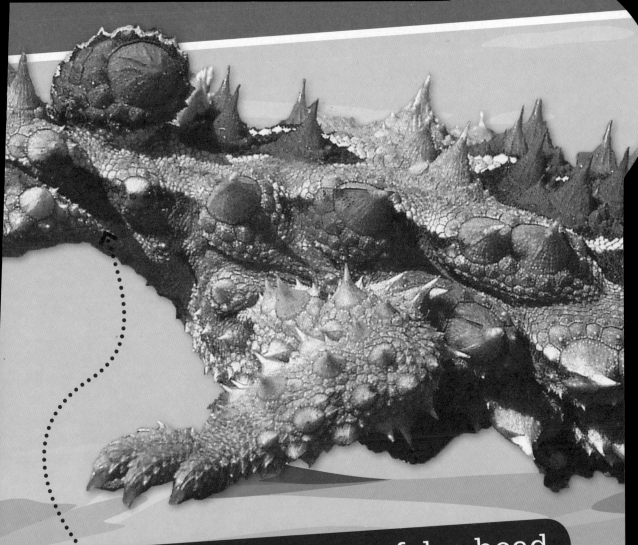

The thorny devil has a false head on its back. When it is threatened, **it hides its real head** between its legs, and shows the false head to its attacker. #0779

171

11 CHAMELEON FACTS

There are **80** different species of chameleon. Half of these live on the **island of Madagascar.**

#0780

Chameleons **change color** depending on their mood or temperature.

#0781

Male chameleons are usually more colorful than females.

#0782

The feet of a chameleon are shaped like tongs, or pincers, allowing them to grip firmly onto the branches of trees.

#0783

With eyes on each side of its head, a chameleon can look in two directions at once. #0784

The **Brookesia micra** is less than an inch long—small enough to stand on the head of a match. #0785

Its eyes can swivel 180 degrees in any direction. #0786

Chameleons have no ears, but they can still sense vibrations in the air. #0787

The egg of a Parson's chameleon can take up to two years to hatch. #0788

A chameleon's tongue can be up to twice as long as its body. #0789

In less than a tenth of a second, a chameleon's tongue can shoot out and snare a buzzing insect. #0790

173

7 FACTS ABOUT Iguanas

Iguanas are **herbivores,** but they may eat the occasional insect as a **snack.**
#0791

In Belize, iguana meat is considered a delicacy. It is known as **BAMBOO CHICKEN.**
#0792

GREEN IGUANAS spend nearly their **WHOLE LIVES IN TREES,** coming to the ground only to lay their eggs.
#0793

Iguanas have been known to survive falls of up to 5 ft—that's the equivalent of a five-story building!
#0794

174

Iguanas have a **"third eye"** in the tops of their heads that is sensitive to changes in light. This helps them to **detect predators** above them. #0795

Male iguanas
bob their heads
to show that they are dominant. #0796

They use their sharp **tails** to drive off predators by whipping them. #0797

175

10 FACTS ABOUT
crocodiles

Crocodiles can swim at up to 15 mph. #0798

They do not use their legs to swim, but push themselves forward by swishing their tails from side to side. #0799

On land, crocodiles crawl on their bellies. When they want to move quickly, they hold their bodies above the ground in a movement called a **"high walk."** #0800

Just before they hatch, baby crocodiles call out to their mothers from inside their eggs. This lets the mother know to come and guard them. #0801

Crocodiles have another set of teeth in their jaws ready to replace a lost or broken one.
#0803

Saltwater crocodiles can slow their heart rate down to **3 beats per minute.** #0802

The Nile crocodile can grow up to **20 ft long.** #0804

Crocodiles live for a very long time. A freshwater crocodile at the **Australia Zoo** called **Mr. Freshy** is thought to be **130 years old.** #0805

Crocodiles can't chew, so they swallow stones to help grind the food in their stomachs. #0806

The stones also make crocs heavier and help them stay underwater. #0807

10 FACTS ABOUT **ALLIGATORS** AND CAIMANS

An alligator can survive for a year **WITHOUT FOOD.**
#0808

Very occasionally alligators are born **completely white.** There are only about 12 white alligators in the world. #0810

Alligators are only found in **CHINA** and the **U.S.** #0809

Alligators sometimes **turn black** when they get older. #0812

When an alligator's **mouth is shut,** you can't see its teeth, but when a crocodile's mouth is shut, its teeth **stick out** of the sides. #0811

The sex of **baby caimans** is decided by the temperature of the nest. At some temperatures, the eggs all hatch as females. At others, they all hatch as males. #0813

Under a bright light, a caiman's eyes are a vivid **RUBY RED.** #0814

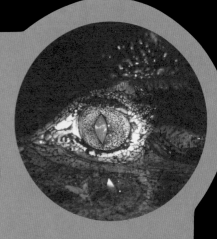

The **musky caiman** is the smallest animal in the family Crocodilia, to which crocodiles and alligators all belong. **Caimans grow to just over 10 ft long.** #0815

Caimans have been known to **EAT EACH OTHER.** #0816

The *gharial* (which lives along rivers in India) uses its extremely **long, thin snout** and **daggerlike teeth** to **SNAP UP FISH.** #0817

179

10 CONSTRICTOR SNAKE FACTS

Constrictor snakes **can stretch their jaws** to swallow large prey whole. In 2012, an African python was **filmed devouring the largest-recorded prey**—an entire wildebeest.
#0818

Reticulated **pythons** have been known to attack **human children** and teenagers, **squeezing** them to death, and swallowing them feet-first. #0819

Female **CARPET PYTHONS** in **WESTERN AUSTRALIA** grow up to four times larger than the males.
#0820

The name

anaconda

comes from a Tamil word meaning **"elephant killer."**
#0821

Female anacondas give birth to more than 40 live babies at a time. #0822

It takes nearly a week for a boa constrictor to digest a meal.
#0823

Boas

can **sense vibrations** in the air with their jaw bones. #0824

The **GREEN ANACONDA** is the heaviest snake. It can weigh 550 lb— as much as three large humans. #0825

Just before it sheds its skin, a boa constrictor's eyes go cloudy blue. Boas have **SCALES OVER THEIR EYES,** and the clouding occurs as the scales begin to come loose. #0826

The longest snake ever measured was a **reticulated python.** Its body was **33 FT LONG**—that's more than double the length of an average family car.
#0827

9 VENOMOUS snake facts

Venomous snakes have fangs like hypodermic needles. The venom runs through the middle of the fang, and is delivered straight into the bloodstream of the victim. #0828

The bite of an inland taipan contains enough venom to kill **100 people.** #0829

Burrowing asps can move each fang separately as they bite their victims. #0830

Flying snakes glide from tree to tree for up to **330 ft.** They flatten their bodies to catch as much air as possible. #0831

There are more than **10,000** Indian cobra attacks on humans every year in India. #0832

In California, rattlesnakes bite people more than **800 times a year.** #0833

The rattle in a rattlesnake's tail is made from skin from past molts. #0834

Unless it is treated immediately, the bite from a black mamba is almost always fatal to humans. #0835

Rather than hissing, the king cobra makes a growling sound. #0836

7 sea snake facts

There are **62 SPECIES** of sea snake in the Indian and Pacific oceans.

#0837

The most VENOMOUS

sea snake is the **Belcher's sea snake.** Its bite does not hurt, but it is likely to kill you within **a few minutes.**

#0838

The dangerous beaded sea snake can **kill eight people with just three drops of venom.** Fortunately, its fangs are too short to bite through a diving suit.

#0841

Sea snakes can hold their breath below water for up to 2 hours.

#0839

The olive sea snake can "see" objects using light receptors in its tail.

#0840

Many sea snakes defend themselves by spraying out a **stinky, musky liquid,** rather than by biting a predator. #0842

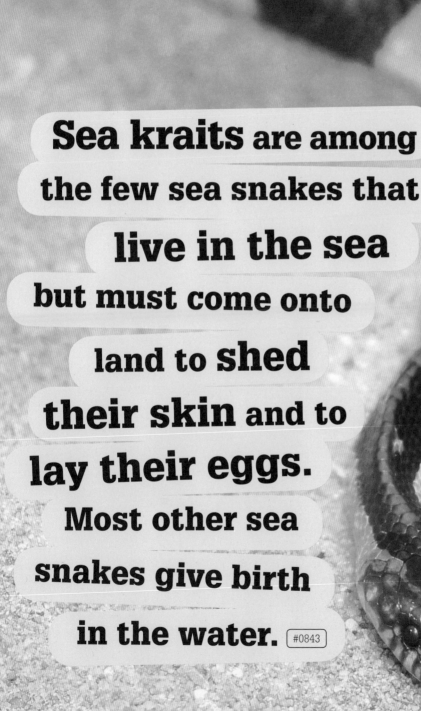

Sea kraits are among the few sea snakes that **live in the sea** but must come onto land to **shed their skin** and to **lay their eggs.** Most other sea snakes give birth in the water. #0843

185

9

turtles
and
tortoises
facts

Many turtles live in the oceans. Tortoises are a kind of turtle that lives on land.
#0844

The alligator snapping turtle lures fish using its tongue, which **looks like a tasty worm.**
#0846

A turtle's shell has about **60 different bones** in it.
#0845

Turtles have been around on Earth for **at least 220 million years.**
#0847

Turtles do not have teeth. Instead, they have **sharp beaks** to tear their food.
#0848

Green turtles **return to the same beach where they hatched** to lay their own eggs.
#0849

One leatherback turtle was tracked swimming **12,400 mi** from Indonesia to the U.S.
#0850

Desert tortoises spend **95%** of their time in burrows nearly 6 ft underground.
#0851

The hingeback tortoise has a hinge at the back of its shell that allows it to close its shell and protect its legs and tail from predators.
#0852

7 GIANT TORTOISE
FACTS

Giant tortoises can weigh up to

660 LB

—as much as four adult humans. #0853

A giant tortoise that died in India in 2006 is thought to have been

255 YEARS OLD.

#0854

The oldest known giant tortoise alive today celebrated its

170th

birthday in 2013. #0855

It is hard to know how old some giant tortoises are as they **outlive the humans who look after them.** #0856

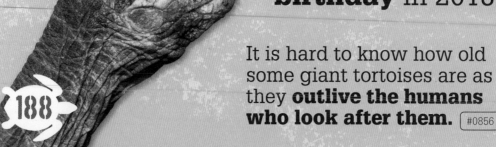

Today, giant tortoises are only found on small tropical islands such as the **SEYCHELLES** in the Indian Ocean and the **GALÁPAGOS** in the Pacific Ocean. #0857

Galápagos   Seychelles

Lonesome George

was the last known Pinta Island tortoise. When he died in 2012 **aged about 100,** the species became extinct.

#0858

Giant tortoise eggs are about the size of a tennis ball.

#0859

Tuataras are **"LIVING FOSSILS"**— they have hardly changed since their nearest relatives died out **60 MILLION YEARS AGO.** #0860

Tuataras are only found in **New Zealand.** #0861

They became **extinct** on the main islands of New Zealand about 200 years ago, and survive only on the smaller islands. #0862

The name **"TUATARA"** comes from a Maori word meaning **"SPINY BACK."** #0863

In 2009, a male tuatara called Henry, kept at Southland Museum in New Zealand, became a father at the age of **111.** #0864

190

Tuataras are active at night, but their hatchlings are active during the day, probably in order to avoid the adults, which are known to eat the hatchlings. #0865

BABY TUATARAS
have a "third eye" on the tops of their heads. Scientists are not sure what it's for. #0866

Tuataras do not have true teeth, but rather sharp projections of jaw bone— **A FEATURE NOT SEEN IN ANY OTHER REPTILE.** #0867

As they get older, the points on their **jaw bones** wear away, and their diet changes from geckos and skinks to **softer prey** such as worms and slugs. #0868

Air temperatures of more than 82°F can be fatal to tuataras because they have a **lower body temperature** than most other reptiles. #0869

191

REPTILES

FACTFILE

AMAZING **REPTILES**

Snakes are all descended from **four-legged lizards.**
#0872

Reptiles are found on every continent ...

... **except** Antarctica.
#0870

REPTILES do not **SWEAT.**
#0871

Reptiles are **cold-blooded,** meaning that they must warm up in the sun before they become active.
#0873

WEIRD BUT TRUE

In the U.S., **13 million** reptiles are kept as pets.
#0874

Spitting cobras **squirt** venom into their victims' eyes to blind them.
#0875

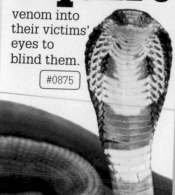

In the U.S., more people die from **bee stings** than from **snakebites.**
#0876

A black rat snake was once born with **TWO HEADS.** It lived for 20 years.
#0877

Some prehistoric snakes grew as long as a bus.

#0878

The leatherback sea turtle has a bendy, rubbery shell.
#0879

REPTILE **BEHAVIOR**

In order to grow, snakes **must molt their OLD SKIN.** #0880

The slender-snouted crocodile is the only crocodile that **climbs trees.** #0881

THE FLYING DRAGON
lizard glides through the air using two large flaps of skin. It steers with its tail. #0883

MARINE IGUANAS
dive up to 50 ft in the oceans to feed on algae.

#0882

DANGEROUS REPTILES

CROCODILES often **sleep with their mouths wide open**. This stops them from overheating. #0884

About **30 percent** of snakes are venomous. Of those, only about 5 percent are **a danger to humans.** #0885

Worldwide, 2.5 million people are bitten by snakes every year. #0886

TWO THIRDS of all the snakebites on humans in Africa are made by PUFF ADDERS. #0887

To scare off many **PREDATORS** the frilled lizard opens a large frill on its neck to make it look bigger than it really is. #0888

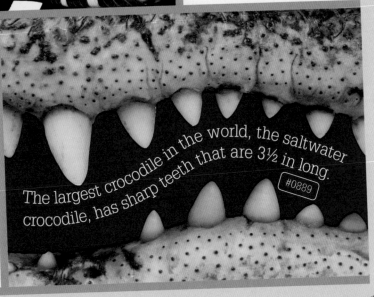
The largest crocodile in the world, the saltwater crocodile, has sharp teeth that are 3½ in long. #0889

AMPHIBIANS

11 FACTS ABOUT FROGS

Frogs don't drink water—they absorb it **through their skin.** #0891

Every frog call is unique to its species. Some sound like a croak, others like a whistle or the chirp of a bird. #0892

A frog completely **sheds its skin** about once a week, and usually **eats it.** #0893

A group of frogs is **called an army.** #0894

When frogs **hibernate,** their bones grow a new layer. You can tell how old a frog is **by counting the growth rings** on its bones. #0895

196.

Some frogs can

JUMP

20 times their own body length.
That is like a human jumping

100 FEET. #0896

Frogs need to hear **underwater**
and on land so, **unlike humans,**
they do not have **external ear parts.** #0897

When a frog **SWALLOWS ITS PREY,** it blinks. This pushes its eyeballs down on top of its mouth to help **PUSH THE FOOD DOWN ITS THROAT**. #0898

A **tornado can suck water** high into the air. If that water contains frogs, it may **rain frogs** some time later. #0899

Frogs and toads have a life cycle that progresses through three stages: **egg, larva,** and **adult.** This can take as little as **12 weeks.** #0900

The common frog catches prey with its **long tongue.** When not needed the tongue stays **rolled up inside its mouth.** #0901

197

6 FACTS ABOUT TOADS

Toads have **shorter legs** than frogs. They **WALK** but do not **HOP.** #0902

Toads do not have teeth, but most frogs do. #0903

A group of toads is called a **knot.** #0904

Most toads burrow beneath the dirt in the daytime, and come out **at night** to feed on insects. #0905

Toads are often killed on roads. In some countries, **toad tunnels** have been built under roads so that **toads can cross safely.** #0906

Many toads look like they're covered in **WARTS,** but they're not. Their bumpy skin helps them to blend in with their environment. #0907

199

7 TREE FROG
FACTS

Tree frogs **keep moist** by **sitting in pools of water** in leaves. #0908

The White's tree frog has such **a tendency to get fat** that it is also known as the **dumpy frog.** #0909

Rather than webbed feet, like other frogs, tree frogs have **sticky pads on their feet** for climbing. #0910

The red-eyed tree frog has a green body with yellow and blue striped sides, and orangey-red feet. **It flashes its brightly colored parts to scare off predators.** #0911

200

The tiny green tree frog of North America has a call like the bark of a dog. #0912

The **waxy monkey tree frog** produces a sticky substance to keep its body from drying out in the high trees of the Amazon. #0913

Its skin contains a **powerful drug** used by Amazonian tribes in rituals. It makes people see things that are not there. #0914

201

9 FACTS ABOUT POISONOUS FROGS AND TOADS

Some Australian frogs create their own insect repellent. It smells like ROTTEN MEAT. #0915

The only animal brave enough to eat the golden poison dart frog is a snake called *Leimadophis epinephelus*, which is immune to its poison. #0917

The **golden poison dart frog** is the most toxic vertebrate on Earth. It is only 2 in long, but it contains **enough poison to kill 10 adults.** #0916

The **blue-jeans frog** has a **red body with blue legs.** It looks like it is wearing denim jeans, hence its name. #0918

Poisonous frogs get much of their poison from the ALKALINE-RICH **ants** and other bugs **that they eat.** #0919

202

The **Chilean four-eyed frog** has a pair of eyespot marks on its backside. They are actually POISON GLANDS, **not eyes.** #0920

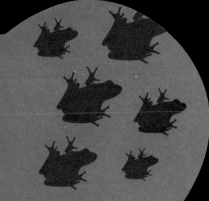

The wartlike glands behind **toads' ears** are dangerous—they can **squirt poison at predators.** #0921

The **FIRE-BELLIED TOAD** has a **red and black belly** that it displays to predators to show them that its **skin is poisonous.** #0922

The **CANE TOAD** was introduced to Australia from South America **TO PREY ON CANE BEETLES,** which were destroying the sugar crop. However, it has multiplied so much that it has become a **MAJOR PEST.** #0923

13 FACTS ABOUT SALAMANDERS

There are only about **550 SPECIES** of salamander, compared to more than **5,500** species of lizard. #0924

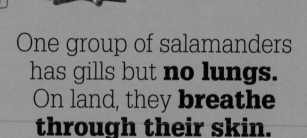

Most salamanders breathe with lungs above water, and with gills underwater. #0925

One group of salamanders has gills but **no lungs. On land, they breathe through their skin.** #0926

The **spotted salamander hides in forest foliage.** It is very hard to find, despite having bright yellow spots. #0927

Land-based salamanders **flick out their long tongues** to catch food. It takes about **10 milliseconds** to catch a fly. #0928

Each individual spotted salamander has its own **unique pattern of spots**. #0929

To escape an attack, some salamanders shed their tails. The separated tail then **wiggles** to distract the predator. #0930

Some salamanders can **grow new tails or limbs**. At first, the new part is paler than the rest, but it eventually darkens to match. #0931

Unlike frogs and toads, salamanders make **no sound** at all.
#0932

The Chinese giant salamander is the **largest in the world.** It can weigh up to 145 lb, the equivalent of an average human female.
#0933

It can grow up to

6 ft LONG
—as long as a tall man.
#0934

The **OLM** is a **BLIND** and **TRANSPARENT** salamander. It can survive without food for

10 YEARS.
#0935

The North American **blind salamander** lives in underground streams and caves. The adults have whitish skin, which **covers their eyes.**
#0936

205

6 FACTS ABOUT AXOLOTLS

Roasted axolotl is considered a delicacy in Mexico. #0937

It is found only in **Lake Xochimilco** and surrounding canals near Mexico City. #0939

The axolotl is a unique **salamander** that keeps its larval features, including **feathery gills** and a dorsal fin, as an adult. #0938

The axolotl feeds on **mollusks, worms, insect larvae, crustaceans,** and **fish.**

#0940

Axolotls can be **aggressive** toward each other. Larger axolotls sometimes **eat smaller ones,** and similar-sized axolotls sometimes eat each other's limbs.

#0942

Axolotls can not only **regrow limbs and tails,** they can also regenerate damaged parts of their **brain and other organs.**

#0941

12 FACTS ABOUT NEWTS

Newts spend their lives on land, returning to water to breed. #0943

The **great crested newt** can grow to **7 in long**—twice as big as some newts. #0944

Male newts perform **courtship rituals** such as fanning their tails, to attract females. #0945

Newts can grow new limbs, eyes, hearts, and jaws. #0946

The great crested newt is a **PROTECTED SPECIES** in the U.K., and you need a license to handle one. #0947

In the mating season, the male great crested newt **develops a large wavy crest** on his back. #0948

When newts come out of the water after breeding, they can travel up to

½ mi

on land looking for food such as worms and beetles.
#0949

The **Japanese fire belly newt** can **regenerate** its **eye lens** up to **18 times** during its lifetime. #0950

Newts **mate without touching** each other. #0951

Many newts have
POISONOUS SKINS
as a defense against
PREDATORS.
#0952

Palmate newts got their name because their feet look like **human hands.** #0953

The rough-skinned newt produces **enough poison to kill an adult human,** but it would only be harmful if the newt was eaten.
#0954

10 FACTS ABOUT
Caecilians

A caecilian is often confused with a worm, but it is actually a kind of amphibian. #0955

A caecilian's skin is made up of ring-shaped segments that encircle its entire body. #0956

Unlike a worm, a caecilian has a skull and a backbone. #0957

Caecilians have tiny eyes and very poor vision. They spend most of their time underground where there is no light. #0958

Some species of caecilians have **no lungs,** and may breathe entirely through their skin. #0959

Caecilians have **strong skulls** that help them to burrow underground in wet, tropical areas. #0960

They have a pair of **tentacles on their faces** that can sniff out food. #0961

A mother feeds her babies by allowing them to scrape skin off her body and eat it. #0962

Like some other amphibians, caecilians' skin **secretes toxins to deter predators**. #0963

The Sagalla caecilian feels its way about by using tentacles on the sides of its head. #0964

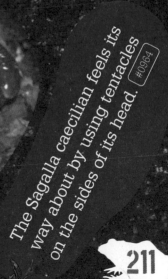

211

9 FACTS ABOUT
Laying eggs

One frogspawn contains about 2,000 eggs.

#0965

Toads lay spawn in strings **up to 3 ft long.**

#0966

Some frog species feed their tadpoles unfertilized eggs if other food is scarce.

#0967

The waxy monkey tree frog lays its eggs in **a jellylike substance rolled up in a leaf.** When the tadpoles emerge, they drop off the leaf into water below.

#0968

The male
Darwin's frog **carries
fertilized eggs in his
vocal pouch.** The tadpoles
develop in the pouch, and
when they are tiny froglets,
they hop out and
swim away.

#0969

If you show
pet frogs **dripping
water,** it might help
them reproduce—they will
think it's the rainy season,
which is when frogs
reproduce in the wild.

#0970

A female newt
lays one egg at a time
on a piece of pond plant.
After laying the egg, she
closes the leaf around it
to protect it.

#0971

The extinct
gastric brooding
frog looked after its
young inside its
stomach. When they were
ready, the **froglets
hopped out of their
mother's mouth.**

#0972

**Some frog eggs
hatch into frogs with
tails, bypassing the
tadpole stage.**

#0973

9 FACTS ABOUT TADPOLES

Frogs, toads, and salamanders start off life as tiny tadpoles. Tadpoles live in water, and breathe using gills. #0974

A tadpole begins as a **DOT INSIDE AN EGG.** As it grows, the tadpole eats its way through the egg jelly. #0975

After **21 days,** the tadpole leaves the jelly, **complete with gills and a long tail.** #0976

Tadpoles eat algae and other plants, but they will also munch on their smaller **BROTHERS AND SISTERS.** #0977

In medieval times, tadpoles were called **porwigles** or **pollywogs.** #0978

Tadpoles of the *Pseudis paradoxa*, or the paradoxical frog, can be up to **10 in long,** but the adult frogs shrink to only about a quarter of this length. #0979

As they grow, the tadpoles **ABSORB** their tails into their bodies. #0980

Tadpoles can survive some **TIME OUT OF WATER** as long as they remain moist. #0981

Finally, tadpoles develop LUNGS and leave the water. #0982

215

AMPHIBIANS FACTFILE

BIG AND SMALL

The world's **largest frog** is the **Goliath frog,** which lives in western Africa. It can grow up to **13 in,** and can weigh **6½ lb**—as heavy as a small baby. #0984

The smallest frog in the **Northern Hemisphere** is the Monte Iberia eleuth, which is less than **3/8 in long.** It is found only in Cuba. #0983

The smallest frog in the **Southern Hemisphere** is the *Paedophryne amauensis* from Papua New Guinea, which is less than **1/4 in long.** #0985

INCREDIBLE AMPHIBIANS

The glass frog has TRANSPARENT skin. You can see its HEART BEATING and its stomach digesting its food. #0987

The Goliath frog has the **biggest leap**—it can jump more than **10 ft.** #0989

Some frogs **confuse predators** with stripes on their backs that appear to split the frog in two when seen from above. #0988

The painted chubby frog is the SAME COLOR as the bark of the tree it likes to cling to, making it almost impossible to see. #0990

AMPHIBIANS were the first animals to live on land. #0986

Horned frogs have a projecting flap, or **"HORN"** of skin, above each eye. #0991

AMPHIBIAN **BEHAVIOR**

The **BARRED LEAF FROG**

has little stripes under its legs that appear to flash when it runs. #0992

Male salamanders become a **BRIGHTER** color during the mating season in order to attract females. #0993

Some frogs can change their color according to **changes in light,** moisture, temperature, or their own mood. #0994

WEIRD BUT TRUE

Scientists are not sure whether the Chilean Darwin's frog is **EXTINCT.** It has rarely been seen since the 1980s, but perhaps it is just very shy! #0996

The caratophrys frog is also known as **the PAC-MAN frog** for its resemblance to the video game character. #0997

Amphibians have **many predators,** but their worst enemy is often **pollution** because they absorb harmful **toxins** through their skin. #0995

MALE FROGS are often more colorful than females. The males can use their appearance to attract females. #0998

The **WOOD FROG** of North America freezes solid during winter, only to come alive again in spring. #0999

AXOLOTLS

must be kept on their own as pets. If you keep more than one in a tank, they will eat each other. #1000

INDEX

223

ACKNOWLEDGMENTS

t = top, b = bottom, l = left, r = right, c = center

1t Didier Descouens/Creative Commons Attribution-Share Alike, 1b Michael Elliott/Dreamstime.com, 4t Peter Wollinga/Shutterstock.com, 4c istockphoto.com, 4b Quartl/Creative Commons Attribution-Share Alike, 5t ThePalmer/istockphoto.com, 5c Ryan M. Bolton/ Shutterstock.com, 5b Number One/Shutterstock.com, 6-7 Setaphong Tantanawat/Shutterstock.com, 8-9 tristan tan/Shutterstock.com, 8br Nacho Such/Shutterstock.com, 9tr Anton_Ivanov/Shutterstock.com, 10l Peter Wollinga/Shutterstock.com, 11tr Hill2k/Shutterstock.com, 12tl Maksim Shmeljov/Shutterstock.com, 13t Maros Bauer/Shutterstock.com, 14-15 Mashe/Shutterstock.com, 16tr Eduard Kyslynskyy/Shutterstock.com, 17 Steffen Foerster/Shutterstock.com, 18-19 tomashko/Shutterstock.com, 20b David Steele/Shutterstock.com, 21tr Colin Edwards Wildside/Shutterstock.com, 21b davidstockphoto/ Shutterstock.com, 22-23b worldwildlifewonders/Shutterstock.com, 23tr clearviewstock/Shutterstock.com, 24tl mark higgins/Shutterstock.com, 25br Patsy A. Jacks/Shutterstock.com, 26-27b Chris Howey/Shutterstock.com, 28-29 George Dolgikh/Shutterstock.com, 30b Stu Porter/Shutterstock. com, 31tr Villers Steyn/Shutterstock.com, 31cr Johann Swanepoel/Shutterstock.com, 32c Eric Isselee/Shutterstock.com, 32bl Steffen Foerster/ Shutterstock.com, 33t Roman Klementschitz/Creative Commons Attribution-Share Alike, 33bl Stephen Dalton/Nature PL, 34t Emi/Shutterstock.com, 35t Ahturner/Shutterstock.com, 35b Daniel Rose/Shutterstock.com, 36tl lightpoet/Shutterstock.com, 36br Steve Bower/Shutterstock.com, 37t Cusson/ Shutterstock.com, 38-39 Ronnie Howard/Shutterstock.com, 41 Fred Goldstein/Shutterstock.com, 42bl lighttraveler/Shutterstock.com, 43tr Molly Marshal/Shutterstock.com, 43br Erik Mandre/Shutterstock.com, 44-45 AnetaPics/Shutterstock.com, 46bl Wassana Mathipikhai/Shutterstock.com, 47bl Ivan Kuzmin/Shutterstock.com, 47br Sandstein/Creative Commons Attribution, 48-49 Sarah Cheriton-Jones/Shutterstock.com, 48tc Cool Kengzz/ Shutterstock.com, 48tr Christian Musat/Shutterstock.com, 48bl Henk Bentlage/Shutterstock.com, 48br Iakov Filimonov/Shutterstock.com, 49br Daniel Alvarez/Shutterstock.com, 50-51 Qidian/Dreamstime.com, 53br Pufferfishy/Dreamstime.com, 54bl Ian Scott/Shutterstock.com, 55tr Photomyeye/ Dreamstime.com, 57br Pr2is/Dreamstime.com, 61br idreamphto/Shutterstock.com, 62-63 Shutterstock.com, 63tr Tom_robbrecht/Dreamstime.com, 64t Robert Taylor/Shutterstock.com, 65 Pixies/Dreamstime.com, 67r Scubaluna/Shutterstock.com, 68bc DJmattaar/Dreamstime.com, 69cl Cbpix/ Dreamstime.com, 69tr istockphoto.com, 70t dtpearson/istockphoto.com, 71b Aleynikov Pavel/Shutterstock.com, 72 all LebendKulturen.de/ Shutterstock.com, 74-75 alterfalter/Shutterstock.com, 76-77 Rich Carey/Shutterstock.com, 79tr Cbpix/Dreamstime.com, 79br izarizhar/Shutterstock. com, 80bl Khoroshunova Olga/Shutterstock.com, 80br Jenny/Creative Commons Attribution, 81tl Dzain/Dreamstime.com, 82tr Kletr/Shutterstock. com, 82-83b Paul Cowell/Shutterstock.com, 83tr Alexander R. Jenner/Creative Commons Attribution-Share Alike, 84 NOAA, 84bl Shutterstock.com, 85b Nature Production/Nature PL, 86-87 Nilzer/Dreamstime.com, 86cl bikeriderlondon/Shutterstock.com, 87tr Paul Cowell/Shutterstock.com, 87cr Bozena Fulawaka, 88-89 wonderisland/Shutterstock.com, 90-91Panachai Cherdchucheep/Shutterstock.com, 90-91c, 91t Didier Descouens/ Creative Commons Attribution-Share Alike, 92c Cathy Keifer, 94-95c Quartl/Creative Commons Attribution-Share Alike, 95tr Peter Factors/ Dreamstime.com, 96-97t paulrommer/Shutterstock.com, 97cl Geoff Chalice//Creative Commons Attribution-Share Alike, 97br Bertrand man/Creative Commons Attribution-Share Alike, 98-99 Galleria/Dreamstime.com, 98t Pan Xunbin/Shutterstock.com, 99tr Randi mal/Shutterstock.com, 100tl, b, 101t Eric Isselee/Shutterstock.com, 100cr, 101bl, cr Peter Waters/Shutterstock.com, 101cl Takahashi/Creative Commons Attribution-Share Alike, 102b Craig Taylor/Shutterstock.com, 103t Kevin Dyer/istockphoto.com, 103c Eric Isselee/Dreamstime.com, 104br JAddams1776, 105t reptiles4all/Shutterstock.com, 106 arlindo/istockphoto.com, 107t rimmer/shutterstock.com, 107b Bjørn Christian Torrissen/Creative Commons Attribution-Share Alike, 108-109 smuay/Shutterstock.com, 110-111 Tomatito/Shutterstock.com, 112bl Amaritz/Dreamstime.com, 114-115 Dreamstime. com, 115tr Ecophoto/Dreamstime.com, 116 Cathy Keifer/Shutterstock.com, 117 Rob Hainer/Shutterstock.com, 119b 3drenderings/Shutterstock.com, 120tl, 120-121c, 120tc, 121bl, 120-121tc Marina Jay/Shutterstock.com, 121bl, 121tr xpixel/Shutterstock.com, 122-123 dcwcreations/Shutterstock.com, 122cr Eduard Kyslynskyy/Shutterstock.com, 123tc szefei/Shutterstock.com, 123br Jefras/Dreamstime.com, 124-25 Syllabub/CC Attribution-Share Alike, 126c Subbotina Anna /Shutterstock, 126b Tim Laman/National Geographical Stock/Nature pl, 127t Johannes Gerhardus Swanepoel/ Dreamstime.com, 127b Roberto A Sanchez/Istockphoto, 128-29 Kiyoshi Takahase Segundo/Dreamstime.com, 129 Charlesjsharp/ CC Attribution, 130 Ingrid Taylar/ CC Attribution, 131 Michael Gwyther-Jones/ CC Attribution, 132t SantiPhotoSS/ Shutterstock, 132c Peter Massas/ CC Attribution, 133t Daniel Alvarez/Shutterstock, 133b Anthony Hathaway/Dreamstime.com, 134 Gerrit_de_Vries/Shutterstock, 135 Chris Zwaenepoel/Dreamstime. com, 136 ajman/Shutterstock, 138t Anders Nyberg/Shutterstock, 138b Mogens Trolle/Shutterstock, 139 Jiri Hera/Shutterstock, 140 Joseph Scott Photography/Shutterstock, 141 Sokolov Alexey/Shutterstock, 142 Georgios Alexandris/Shutterstock, 143 Roy Longmuir/ Dreamstime.com, 145 tratong/Shutterstock, 145–146 Jan Martin Will/Shutterstock, 145 Armin/Dreamstime.com, 149l bluelake/Shutterstock, 149r Eric Isselee/ Shutterstock, 150 AdStock RF/Shutterstock, 151t feathercollector/Shutterstock, 151b john michael evan potter/Shutterstock, 152 Johan Swanepoel/ Shutterstock, 153c Carlos Arranz/Dreamstime.com 153b Steve Weaver/Dreamstime.com, 154 Fotograf77/Dreamstime.com, 155 Luckynick/ Dreamstime.com, 156t panbazil/Shutterstock, 156b Digoarpi/Shutterstock, 157t Arcoss/Dreamstime.com, 157b Eric Isselee/Shutterstock, 158 AlessandroZocc/Shutterstock, 159t Mark Medcalf/Shutterstock, 159c Lee319/Shutterstock, 159b Anton_Ivanov/Shutterstock, 160-161 Yuri2010/ Shutterstock.com, 162tl Teddykebab/Dreamstime.com, 163br Leena Robinson/Shutterstock.com, 164 fivespots/Shutterstock.com, 165 AYImages/ istockphoto.com, 167t Marlin Hams/Creative Commons Attribution, 167br Mark Tipping/Shutterstock.com, 168-169 Ecophoto/Dreamstime.com, 169tr Lodimup/Shutterstock.com, 171t Gassenbach/Dreamstime.com, 172-173 Snowshill/Shutterstock.com, 174bl apiguide/Shutterstock.com, 175tr Stayer/Shutterstock.com, 176-177c Yentafern/Shutterstock.com, 177br Netfalis—Ryan Musser/Shutterstock.com, 178b markrhiggens/ istockphoto.com, 179tr Ryan M.Bolton/Shutterstock.com, 179br Buckskinman/Dreamstime.com, 180b Firman Wahyudin/Shutterstock.com, 181t Starper/Dreamstime.com, 182cl Aussiebluey/Dreamstime.com, 182-183t Chuck Rausin/Shutterstock.com, 182-183b Aleksey Stemmer/ Shutterstock.com, 183tr Dreamstime.com, 183cr DiscoDad/Shutterstock.com, 184b Paul Cowell/Shutterstock.com, 185 Joefoto/Dreamstime.com, 186-187 abcphotosystem/Shutterstock.com, 186bl Ryan M. Bolton/Shutterstock.com, 187cr reptiles4all/Shutterstock.com, 188bl Ryan M. Bolton/ Shutterstock.com, 189tr Pxhidalgo/Dreamstime.com, 190b Undy/Dreamstime.com, 192-193 Olena/Shutterstock.com, 192bl Yuri 2010/Shutterstock. com, 193cl Dennis Donohue/Shutterstock.com, 193br Eric Isselee/Shutterstock.com, 194-195 Eduard Kyslynskyy/Shutterstock.com, 196bl Number One/Shutterstock.com, 197tr Ridgerunner91/Dreamstime.com, 197b sanjals/Dreamstime.com, 198c oe/istockphoto.com, 199 Josh92mac/Shutterstock. com, 200 Dirk Ercken/Shutterstock.com, 201 Cathy Keifer/Dreamstime.com, 202tl reptiles4all/Shutterstock.com, 203c Art_Man/Shutterstock.com, 204t Jdeboer152/Dreasmtime.com, 204bl cristl180884/Shutterstock.com, 205br Matt Jeppson/Shutterstock.com, 206-207 Misulka/Dreamstime.com, 208-209 Dirk Ercken/Shutterstock.com, 209tr Melinda Fawver/Shutterstock.com, 210-211 ifong/Shutterstock.com, 210c Pete Oxford/Nature PL, 211b Hilary Jeffkins/Nature PL, 212-213 AdStockRF/Shutterstock.com, 212c Alessandrozocc/Dreamstime.com, 213 cBert Willaert/Nature PL, 214tr BMJ/Shutterstock.com, 214c Eric Isselee/Shutterstock.com, 214br Dr. Morley Read/Shutterstock.com, 216-217 Eric Isselee/Shutterstock.com, 216tr NASA, 216br Aleksey Stemmer/Shutterstock.com, 217tl Dr. Morley Read/Shutterstock.com, 217br Andrew Burgess/Shutterstock.com